BERNARD SHAW

BERNARD SHAW.
1906.
after the bust by Rodin.

Bernard Shaw

By

Holbrook Jackson

"They haif said.   What say they?   Let thame say."

With four Portraits

London
E. Grant Richards
1907

CONTENTS

LIST OF PORTRAITS

PREFATORY LETTER TO
A. R. ORAGE

MY DEAR ORAGE,—You will remember how, some years ago, we were thrown together by the Fates in that smoky chaos which is known to geographers and others as Leeds. I have a clear recollection of the exact circumstances. It was in a bookshop, into which we had both turned, probably to find in books that community of ideas which we were unable to find locally among men. We were pottering around some shelves containing books of the genus Second-hand, which were set far back in the partial gloom and comparative quietness of the remote end of the shop. We stalked our quarry in that absorbed and dilatory way peculiar to the book-hunter. After a while I heard you throw the intelligence department of the em-

porium out of gear by inquiring for a volume by a modern writer, well enough known among thoughtful people, but evidently a dark continent to Leeds. I had been living in the town some twelve months, and this was the first intimation I had received of any one in the place being interested in the writers who interested me. The Leeds booksellers seemed to exist on theology, the Leeds people on commerce and cricket. I was amazed for a moment. I felt as one who had stumbled accidentally upon a new planet. I made an involuntary movement towards you; my instinct, I remember, was as that of one bent upon catching hold of a thing too good to be missed.

Some days later we were seated together in my house at Headingley, where you found the book to which we owed our acquaintance— and many others duplicating in a series of pleasant coincidences those on your own shelves at Chapel-Allerton. For we soon found that intellectually we had been navigating the same seas and, what is more, using

Prefatory Letter

similar charts. We found that we could cap each other's stories, and that we had touched identical ports in unfamiliar Archipelagoes. Since then we have sailed pretty much together, and have been fortunate in speaking many ships, the language of whose crews answered familiarly with our own. And on this particular occasion, as indeed on many another, we engaged in a mutual retelling of adventures in the perilous seas and faery lands forlorn of the mind and the imagination. We did not find, however, that our minds were alike, we found rather that they were akin. In fact, there were gaps and differences, which I am glad to say exist even now, and which I am also glad to say are a continual source of mutual concern. I rejoice, moreover, to think that our friendship has not been engaged in filling up these gaps—it has accepted them as natural features ; but this does not mean that bridges have not been thrown across. Indeed, you will remember how our first meeting at Headingley was memorable in this respect, for did we not on that occasion build a bridge

from the Orient to the Occident? You left behind you that night, or rather the next morning, for we had talked the night away, a translation of the *Bhagavad Gita*; and you carried under your arm my copy of the first English version of *Thus spake Zarathustra*.

After a while we found others of our kind in Leeds. We discovered, much to our surprise, that hidden in various parts of the city, for the most part unknown to each other, were men and women dreaming similar dreams to ours and thinking like thoughts. Gradually we grew acquainted, and conversations grew into prolonged discussions. We turned quiet corners of local cafés into temporary forums, often extending the lunch-hour in a way quite heretical in Yorkshire. At these talks the name of Bernard Shaw was often heard. We were all more or less familiar with his point of view, for in many ways he had been the touchstone of our acquaintanceship; but this does not mean, as you will remember, that we accepted G.B.S. without demur. On the contrary, we did nothing of the sort, but we at

Prefatory Letter

least recognised in him the most acute and suggestive mind in contemporary English literature. We knew he was a force to be taken into account ; we were unanimous in our belief that only in the vitalised action advocated by him was there any hope for the redemption of a social system which had become a chaos and a desolation, as our urban surroundings constantly reminded us. Out of these meetings was born the Leeds Arts Club, with its contempt of pedantic philosophy and academic art, and its insistence upon the necessity of applying ideas to life. You will not have forgotten how you opened our first session with a lecture on Nietzsche, and how I lectured later on Bernard Shaw. We shall never forget how our little band of members worked, and how the Club flourished ; nor how respectable Leeds at first held back fearing our revolutionary ideas, and then gradually came forward reassured by the excellence of our exhibitions ; and how in turn many of these good people joined the Club and actually became revolutionaries them-

selves. Nor shall we forget how such men as Edward Carpenter, Gilbert Chesterton, Cobden-Sanderson, and W. B. Yeats came long distances to help our cause; and how Bernard Shaw left off rehearsing a play and came down from London to give an address, which set Leeds talking for weeks.

This was a great event, for, as I say, we found in Bernard Shaw what might be called a working problem, and we two at least, though not quite clear upon every detail of the Shavian philosophy, marvelled at the meagre acceptance of Shaw as a leader of thought. It was my constantly expressed irritation at the incapacity of the people I met, and those who expressed themselves in the Press, to comprehend a writer who was as clear as day to me, that prompted you one day to suggest my writing a Shaw monograph—and here it is. I took you at your word, but I fear I took my own time, for the book should have been done at least two years ago. But many things have happened in the meantime. We have pitched our tents in London, for

Prefatory Letter

instance, and our intellectual partnership has been concentrated in a still more practical way in our co-editorship of the *New Age*.

Among the many problems raised by Bernard Shaw there is one that has gradually been forced upon us by the perpetual falling to pieces of critics of all orders at the instigation of each new preface from his pen. Is the Press and public hopelessly stupid, or is Shaw explaining himself into obscurity? Neither you nor I would wish him to cease explaining himself, and there are many with a similar taste. But it is quite evident that what is on the whole clear to us is not clear to a large number of apparently intelligent and always well-meaning people. I don't mean the man-in-the-street ; he does not count in this issue ; he will always take his Shaw in the snippet form kindly provided for him by a benevolent and discriminating Press. I mean the intelligent person whose brain is worthy of a better cause ; the type of mind that still persists in believing Shaw a humorist, a trivial and entertaining dialectician, or even, to use the

latest epithet of the delectable and erudite dramatic critic of *The Times*, a *naïf*. That Shaw is a *naïf* is no reason why he should not also be a sound philosopher. I have never yet been convinced that a recapitulation of the obvious is inconsistent with wisdom ; and, on the other hand, *naïveté* is more often than not the handmaiden of all that is delightful in imaginative work. Shaw has imagination to so great an extent that his philosophic expositions become imaginative literature ; this in itself is so rare a thing among philosophers that it is enough to throw erudite persons out of key. But this does not matter, for the writer who makes essays with deference to erudite and pedantic opinion is also out of our reckoning. His work is neither for all time, nor yet for a day, because it is generally still-born. These people and their works are constitutionally dull, and we, like good Levites, pass by on the other side. But what of those who are not dull, who really belong to the modern movement, but are yet kept on the wrong side of the Bernard Shaw depart-

Prefatory Letter

ment because of G.B.S. ?   Well it is for such that I have written this book, of which you are godfather.

I have deliberately refrained from hair-splitting or from tracking down subtleties of thought to their biological and metaphysical lairs. This would have defeated my purpose by confusing when I wished to make clear. I have tried to link up the main ideas which go to make the problem of Bernard Shaw into what I hope you will find a simple and convincing chain.   All I want now is that readers of my book should not jump at any foolish conclusion as to an endeavour on my part to "place" Shaw ; the time is not yet ripe for such an effort.   Nor do I wish them to prepare themselves for disappointment by anticipating a detailed account of each of his separate works : I am not playing the part of commentator, but of interpreter.   My one aim is to induce people to refuse Shaw on any but first-hand terms—to read him, in short, and not to be content with opinions of him from other sources no matter how exalted.

Bernard Shaw

For I think our experiences tally on this point, that the author of *Man and Superman*, like the author of *Hamlet*, are both more talked about than studied, and I am quite convinced that as the touchstone to the worthiness of our Leeds friends was their attitude towards the former, so the ratio of individuals towards the modern movement of ideas must be gauged by the intelligence of their attitude towards the same person. If Bernard Shaw's work were merely unique, we could all afford to laugh and pass on ; but it is a great deal more than that, it stands in the same relation to our day as the work of Swift did to his day, or Carlyle's to his, and people to-day who are ready to admit the insufficiency of intelligent discrimination then are reminded not to repeat a similar error in judgment now.

Yours always,

HOLBROOK JACKSON.

Mill Hill, N.W.

NOTE

No book is made by one man alone, and I wish those who have helped me in the making of this little work to accept my gratitude. Special mention, however, must be made of Mr. Frederick H. Evans and of Mr. Alvin Langdon Coburn, whose ready permission to copy their splendid photographs of Bernard Shaw has given me an opportunity of making my book more valuable than otherwise it would have been; and I must not forget in this reference M. August Rodin, by whose courtesy the frontispiece of this volume is a photograph of a masterpiece in portrait statuary; and also Mrs. Bernard Shaw, who helped me in the choice of the photographs and lent me copies of her valuable prints. I have to thank also my friends, Frederick Richardson for candid criticism, and A. R. Orage for unwearying help, from the mutual discussion of

Benediction

obscure points to the drudgery of proof-reading. And, finally, I must express my indebtedness to the subject of this monograph himself, for information and suggestions of the utmost value, given in that spirit of generosity familiar to those who know him in private life.

H. J.

I

THE MAN

Just consider my position. Do I receive any spontaneous recognition for the prodigies of skill and industry I lavish on an unworthy institution and a stupid public? Not a bit of it: half my time is spent in telling people what a clever man I am. It is no use merely doing clever things in England. The English do not know what to think until they are coached, laboriously and insistently for years, in the proper and becoming opinion. For ten years past, with an unprecedented pertinacity and obstination, I have been dinning into the public head that I am an extraordinarily witty, brilliant, and clever man. That is now part of the public opinion of England; and no power in heaven or on earth will ever change it. I may dodder and dote; I may potboil and platitudinise; I may become the butt and chopping-block of all the bright, original spirits of the rising generation; but my reputation shall not suffer; it is built up fast and solid, like Shakespear's, on an impregnable basis of dogmatic reiteration.—"Valedictory," *The Saturday Review*, 21st *May*, 1898.

I

THE MAN

THOSE who fly in the face of public opinion and devote themselves to the propaganda of new ideas commonly meet with the same reception. It may, and in fact does, vary from age to age in its outward manifestation, but in essence its sameness is positively monotonous. From execution of the author, down through the steps of censorship and expurgation, to the civilised forms of abuse, the uniform purpose has been suppression. In our own day, downright abuse has lost its fashion in the literary world, and is thoroughly at home only on the political platform. But suppression by silence is still as active and ineffective as suppression has always been ; and, strangely enough, among the very people who

loudly denounce the abusive methods with which, for example, Shelley was greeted by his cultured contemporaries.

There is, however, an exception in these days of an insatiable journalism. If your man of new ideas can only make himself entertaining, and can contrive to tickle the jaded palates of the newspaper readers, he may rely upon being paragraphed into notoriety. Editors will indeed wait upon him cap in hand, and publish his articles with something like a fanfare, reserving, however, to themselves one little right—the right to add an editorial disclaimer of responsibility. "Of course," they say, "So-and-so is very witty and amusing ; his stuff will *sell* ; only let us warn our readers that the editorial 'we' does not take him seriously. He doesn't even take himself seriously."

This suppression by laughter is, in fact, the reception accorded to George Bernard Shaw by most of the English critics. As for the British public, what is wrong with them Shaw has told us. It "is what is wrong with the

prosaic men of all countries—stupidity." In England, Press and public are—prosaic!

But the case of Shaw does not induce pity. There is no immediate danger of his being "snuffed out by an article." There is even much evidence of wilful provocation on his part. He seems sometimes to stand aside after throwing to his critics a more than usually irritating truth, and to watch with amusement their attempts to deal with it. And that very attitude of his adds to their irritation.

Nor is it by any means merely the majority of his readers who find him difficult to appreciate. The "acute but honourable minority" which men of ideas may generally look to command, is in Shaw's case placed often enough in a dilemma. His greatest admirers have their trying moments, when they hesitate between joining the majority and swallowing a gibe directed unmistakably against themselves. For Shaw discourages discipleship: and his would-be disciples receive more chastening than indulgence at his hands. In this respect he would seem to say with Nietzsche:

Follow yourselves and you will find me; follow me and you will lose both me and yourselves. This attitude, however, while thoroughly consistent with the rest of his doctrine, is disconcerting to human nature. It appears like wilfulness. It *is* wilfulness. And when one remembers that wilfulness has been suppressed in most of us from the cradle, it is scarcely surprising that we should be pained and shocked when we find a man who has escaped this discipline. Shaw is, in fact, an *enfant terrible* grown up. His native wilfulness (to call an excellent thing by a bad name) is still as fresh in him as it was in Adam and Eve. And the rest of us are compelled to detest it—because we envy it.

Is Shaw serious, is he sincere? Such questions are naturally raised by the spectacle of a mind that can play with ideas. The English mind finds thinking so very laborious, that it naturally associates easy thinking with superficial thinking. To be able to think, and at the same time to be witty,—that is almost a contradiction in terms for many men. More-

The Man

over, it is so easy to take the wit and let the thought go that Shaw was almost certain to be regarded as a wit first, and as a thinker a long way after. In the same way, there are still people to be found who read Shelley simply, as they say, for his poetry. To them Shelley's ideas are an unwarrantable and, in any case, a negligible superimposition on his poetry. But there is a little malicious misrepresentation as well. The critics choose to forget the serious work Shaw has done in politics, economics, and the like. Few men have worked harder at their ideas than Shaw : and if he is witty, it is not because he is superficial, but because his rare gift of playing with ideas is the sign of mastery long and seriously accomplished.

It is undeniable, however, that Shaw has been largely responsible for the misunderstanding. Explanations seldom really explain, and, as Shaw says, he is nothing if not explanatory. His frank egotism, too, is bewildering in its sincerity. Three parts of all literature is, of course, egotism, only egotism carefully veiled by the use of the third person ; but Shaw

drops the veil—he even calls attention to the fact that he has dropped it—and stands forth nakedly egotistical and still unashamed. If you charge him with self-advertisement, he is not abashed ; on the contrary, he congratulates you on having at last understood what he has told you. "I am ashamed," he says, "neither of my work nor the way it is done. . . . I like explaining its merits to the huge majority who don't know good work from bad. It does them good ; and it does me good, curing me of nervousness, laziness, and snobbishness." If you call him charlatan he promptly agrees, adding, in one of those familiar autobiographical annotations, that he first caught the ear of the British public on a cart in Hyde Park, "not at all as a reluctant sacrifice of my instincts of privacy to political necessity, but because, like all dramatists and mimes of genuine vocation,—I am a natural-born mountebank."

A man who welcomes all the terms meant opprobriously and claims them as his distinguishing merits, is plainly difficult to

understand. His very frankness and sincerity conceal him. But if the charge of insincerity can only be brought against Shaw by the prosaic, this is even more emphatically true of the charge of negation. Many of those who appreciate his ideas as well as his wit complain at times that Shaw is more destructive than constructive. The vast majority of his readers are positively surprised to hear that Shaw has any constructive ideas at all.

The destructive position is practically forced upon men of ideas who follow a century like the nineteenth. It required to be shown beyond shadow of doubt that the nineteenth-century theories of society were hopelessly and tragically wrong. People will not listen to a new theory of society so long as they believe the old theory is right. Hence, the modern reformer is of necessity an iconoclast first and a builder afterwards. But there is plenty of evidence in Shaw's case at least that iconoclasm is followed immediately by construction. Let those who know his books and still doubt this ask themselves what view of society they

gather from Shaw's pages. Unless his readers are singularly lacking in perception, they will be able to describe pretty fully not only the form of society which Shaw conceives, but the type of men and women whom he dreams shall compose it. For Shaw also has his visions, and dreams his dreams; and behind the pages of his most destructive criticism judicious readers can descry the shining outlines of a Utopia resplendent and glorious as any that man has imagined.

Such domestic personalia as is necessary to this work had better be told, as far as possible, in Shaw's own words. There are two reasons for this : one the chance of obtaining a concise picture of the G.B.S. of popular superstition, in the creation of which Bernard Shaw has had no small share, and from which certain critical deductions may be drawn; and secondly because the personal notes scattered about his prefaces and in the columns of the Press are among the most piquant and characteristic of his utterances, and throw a vivid light on the peculiarity of a frankly critical nature that does

The Man

not shrink from turning the X-rays of its analytic power upon itself. This should serve as a consolation to those who, while disliking excessive frankness, make a god of consistency.

He was born in Dublin on 26 July, 1856. He was the third and last child, and only son of George Carr Shaw, of Dublin, for many years an old-style civil servant, who retired on a pension, which he sold, afterwards going into business as a merchant and mill-owner. The enterprise, however, was only moderately successful, owing to limitations of capital and failure to cope with changing commercial conditions. The family was a middle-class one, with all the prejudices and habits of that class. "They talked of ' the Shaws ' as of the Hohenzollerns or Romanoffs," says their famous descendant, but their circumstances must have always bordered on the impecunious. "My father," he says, "was an ineffective, unsuccessful man, in theory a vehement teetotaller, but in practice often a furtive drinker. He might have been a weaker brother of Charles Lamb."

While inheriting none of his father's ineffectuality, G.B.S. must have received some legacy of humour from that "weaker brother of Charles Lamb," for we have an anecdote, simple enough in its way, but illustrating just that self-conscious humour expressed in impulsive anti-climax which the son has turned into a literary weapon of phenomenal power. "When I was a child," G.B.S. tells us, "my father gave me my first dip in the sea in Kelliney Bay. He prefaced it by a very serious exhortation on the importance of learning to swim, culminating in these words : 'When I was a boy of only fourteen, my knowledge of swimming enabled me to save your uncle Robert's life.' Then, seeing I was deeply impressed, he stooped, and added confidentially in my ear, 'And to tell you the truth, I never was so sorry for anything in my life afterwards.' He then plunged into the ocean, enjoyed a thoroughly refreshing swim, and chuckled all the way home."

His mother, who was twenty years younger than her husband, and who is still living

The Man

("and much younger than her children," says her son), was Lucinda Elizabeth Gurly, the daughter of Walter Bagnal Gurly, a country gentleman of Carlow, whose estate G.B.S. inherited, and made solvent out of his literary earnings, on his maternal uncle's death. She evidently supplied whatever capability there was in the home. She must have possessed the determination of purpose which the father lacked; but she was not a domestic genius. Her tastes were an anticipation of those of the comparatively freer woman of to-day. She was self-centred and humane, with a complete indifference to public opinion, which her son has certainly inherited. In fact, Bernard Shaw takes his most definite characteristics from his mother. Her independence, her taste in music, her unromantic attitude towards life, and above all, her energy and perseverance, and that manner of dealing with prejudices by walking straight through them as if they were not there, are the obvious sources of similar features in the genius of the son. She threw all her energy into music, and

33

achieved a distinction as an amateur singer and as the indefatigable lieutenant of an energetic organiser of concerts, oratorios, and even operas in Dublin, which qualified her in later life to earn her own living and her son's as a teacher of singing and a trainer of choirs in London. She came to London ostensibly to help her daughter into the profession of music as a singer, but remained as a teacher of singing first, and later as a conductor of girls' choirs in public schools, a work she continued until she was over seventy. "Even then," Shaw says, "retirement was not easy, as she retained both her vigor and her voice."

Mr. James Huneker, the clever American journalist, author of *Iconoclasts : A Book of Dramatists*, has been persuasively and emphatically reproved by Shaw for making him a kind of Log Cabin to White House hero who "got on" by sheer devotion to the romantic duties of that exalted aim ; and in the preface to *The Irrational Knot* there is a fine tribute to the mother who contributed her energy towards finding the means of subsist-

ence while the son followed the path he had chosen. "I was an able-bodied and able-minded young man in the strength of my youth," says this candid son, "and my family, then heavily embarrassed, needed my help urgently. That I should have chosen to be a burden to them instead was, according to all the conventions of peasant lad fiction, monstrous. Well, without a blush I embraced the monstrosity. I did not throw myself into the struggle for life : I threw my mother into it. I was not a staff to my father's old age : I hung on to his coat-tails." He describes his mother "drudging in her elder years at the art of music" for him, and is ready to recognise this as frankly as he recognises the dependence of the Rev. James Mavor Morrell on Candida. But Mrs. Shaw was obviously no Candida. The son of Candida would have enjoyed very little freedom, however well mothered he might have been. Mrs. Shaw went her own way and allowed her son to go his. They suited one another well in this respect. Mrs. Clandon, in *You Never Can*

Tell, shows how well the author knows the thoroughly humane, able woman whose interests lie outside the home, and who is incommoded by displays of family sentiment. There was probably a good deal of Mrs. Clandon, and certainly nothing of Candida, in Mrs. Shaw. And there is a good deal of Mrs. Shaw in her son. That is why he will not suffer " James Huneker or any romanticist to pass him off " as a peasant boy qualifying for a chapter in Smiles' *Self-Help*, or a good son supporting a helpless mother, instead of a " stupendously selfish artist leaning with the full weight of his hungry body on an energetic and capable woman."

Of Bernard Shaw's two sisters, one, named Agnes, died in 1876, just as she came of age ; the other, Miss Lucy Carr Shaw, the cause of her mother's coming to London, became a professional singer, and now lives in retirement in Germany. She has made some excursions into print, her best-known work in this sphere being a series of excellent letters on the education of a girl, recently published

under the title, *Five Letters of the House of Kildonnel*.

As to Shaw's education and early training, the ensuing results have proved them fortunate to the curve of growth which nature meant him to follow, for of education in the usual sense of the word he had little, and therefore little to unlearn. "I never learnt anything at school," he says, "a place where they put Cæsar and Horace into the hands of small boys, and expected the result to be an elegant taste and knowledge of the world. I took refuge in total idleness at school, and picked up at home, quite unconsciously, a knowledge of that extraordinary literature of modern music, from Bach to Wagner, which has saved me from being at the smallest disadvantage in competition with men who only know the grammar and mispronunciation of the Greek and Latin poets and philosophers. For the rest, my parents went their own way and let me go mine. Thus the habit of freedom, which most Englishmen and Englishwomen of my class never acquire and

never let their children acquire, came to me naturally."

When quite a small boy a clerical uncle, the Rev. William George Carroll, Vicar of St. Bride's, Dublin, who, it is interesting to note, was the first Protestant parson in Ireland to declare for Home Rule, taught him some Latin grammar. Afterwards he was sent to the Wesleyan Connexional School, now known as Wesley College, in Stephen's Green. In Ireland the Protestant does not draw the same distinction between Nonconformist and Established Churches as in England. There the distinction is the broad one between Protestantism and Roman Catholicism, and that is how it was possible for the young Bernard Shaw to find himself under the tuition of Wesleyans. In reference to this matter he says, "I was sent, with many boys of my own denomination, to a Wesleyan school, where the Wesleyan catechism was taught without the least protest on the part of the parents, although there was so little presumption in favour of any boy there being a Wesleyan,

that if all the Church boys had been with-
drawn at any moment the school would have
become bankrupt." But although of Protestant family, Shaw was never confirmed a
member of the Church, and there was nearly
a hitch in his baptism, for the appointed godfather failed to appear at the font, and his re-
sponsibilities had to be somewhat hurriedly
assumed by the sexton.

He remained at the Wesleyan Connexional
School for several years, where he learnt so
little that on being examined by the uncle who
previously had taught him Latin, his ignorance
of the usual scholastic knowledge was made
apparent. But he knew something of more
value : he had acquired the beginnings of
that deep knowledge of literature, music, and
painting, which has been of such use to him
ever since ; and he would have known much
more even at this early age had his own in-
clinations been consulted, and his education
not "interrupted by schooling." After this
experience he says : "I was experimented on
desultorily in a few other schools, but the

result was the same—I learnt nothing; and the value received by my parents for their expenditure was simply the getting me out of the way for half the day. I was always a day boy, and had no experience of boarding schools. At the Wesleyan Connexional it was a point of honour for the boarders and day boys to despise one another. We called each other 'the skinnies,' the implication being that we were inadequately fed at school, or in the home, as the case might be. I was tolerated in school solely as a source of income to the establishment. In an uncommercial system of education I should have been thrown into the street as an unemployable. I was an unmitigated nuisance until the phenomenon described in the first act of *Man and Superman* as the dawning of the moral passion took place; and by that time I was nearing the end of my schooldays, which I look back on as the most completely wasted and mischievous part of my life."

The inclination to write was never a consuming desire. At the same time, when he

BERNARD SHAW
1879

was a small boy he "concocted a short story and sent it to some boys' journal," but the definite wish to write was never present, "any more than I ever felt inclined to breathe." He wished to draw, and Michelangelo was his boyish ideal. When he had grown out of the "earlier impulse towards piracy and highway robbery" he inclined towards a wicked baritone in an opera. Summing the matter up he says, "No, I never wanted to write. I know, of course, the value and the scarcity of the literary faculty (though I think it overrated), but I still don't want it"; adding in sly anticlimax, "You cannot want a thing and have it too." So what came by nature grew by the help of indomitable perseverance and untiring energy.

This literary energy which usually produces early works, he assures us, was worked off in the correspondence of a romantic friendship with Edward McNulty, a schoolfellow, who afterwards wrote the Irish novels *Misther O'Ryan* and *The Son of a Peasant*. This correspondence, which one may be excused for

hoping the Fates have preserved, covered the ages from fifteen to twenty, when the occasion of the visit of the American evangelists, Moody and Sankey, to Dublin, where Shaw, then a clerk, was employed in Irish land agency (of all employments for a future revolutionist!), caused his first appearance in print. "I went to hear them," he says. "I was wholly unmoved by their eloquence, and felt bound to inform the public that I was, on the whole, an atheist. My letter was solemnly printed in *Public Opinion*, to the extreme horror of my numerous uncles."

This early publicity in the form of a letter to the editor of a journal is strictly in keeping with the ensuing order of things, and this literary and propagandist predilection is one of his most persistent characteristics. But the incident of Moody and Sankey and *Public Opinion* was not the first offence, for there was imminent peril of the tradition being established some years before, and it was presumably only the fact of the peculiar wit which we know to-day being born out of its due

The Man

time that prevented its baptism of print as early as the year 1871. For in the *Vaudeville Magazine*, which described itself as "a Monthly Journal of Fact, Fiction, Fun, and Fancy," and which was evidently beloved of the gods, for it died at the tender age of six months, there occurs the following among the Editorial Replies, under date September, 1871, G. B. Shaw (Torca Cottage, Torca Hill, Dalkey, Co. Dublin, Ireland) : "You should have registered your letter ; such a combination of wit and satire ought not to have been conveyed at the ordinary rate of postage. As it was, your arguments were so weighty we had to pay *two pence* extra for them." Here, probably, is the earliest public reference to that diablerie which has become a common object of the Press, and the editor of 1871 was evidently as bewildered as so many editors and others have been since.

He left school at the age of fourteen, and from the age of fifteen to twenty he did ordinary office work. He entered the office of Mr. Charles Uniacke Townshend, of Dublin, with the object of learning the business of

land agency, and remained there for some five years. He must have shown skill in his work, for when he was sixteen a position of trust occupied by a man of responsible years in the office suddenly became vacant, and to meet the emergency Shaw was thrust into the post for a day and held it for four years, when he "simply jumped overboard" by resigning his appointment and throwing himself on his mother's hands in settling in London in 1876. Here is his own characteristic description of this event and its subsequent result. "At the age of sixteen I was thrust on an emergency into a grown man's post which was the most responsible, both as to money and other matters, in the whole office; and not all my distaste for it, nor my utter want of interest in and consequently comprehension of the business, availed to displace me afterwards. One of the remorses of my life is for my ridiculous anger with my father because he, poor man, with a view to helping me to commercial employment in London (which I specially dreaded finding), went to Mr. Town-

The Man

shend and obtained from him a testimonial in such handsome terms that any one reading it would have supposed that I was born to be cashier of the Bank of England." But he did not give up the habit of looking to an office for employment until 1879. He would not have it supposed that because he is a man of letters he never tried to earn an honest living. "I began," he says, "to commit that sin against my nature when I was fifteen, and persevered, from youthful timidity and diffidence, until I was twenty-three. My last attempt was in 1879, when a company was formed in London to exploit an ingenious invention by Mr. Thomas Alva Edison—a much too ingenious invention, as it proved, being nothing less than a telephone of such stentorian efficiency that it bellowed your most private communications all over the house instead of whispering them with some sort of discretion." In what capacity the future author of *Man and Superman* served this concern does not transpire from his own confession, but it appears that from the accident

of his possessing some knowledge of physics and chemistry, and thereby of being the only member of the establishment who could give "the current scientific explanation of telephony," he often found himself discharging the duties of official lecturer to the company in place of the gentleman who was specifically engaged for that purpose, but "whose strong point was pre-scientific agriculture." He is persuaded thereby that he laid the foundation of Mr. Edison's London reputation. In these early experiences as a lecturer he was often amused at the half-concealed incredulity of the visitors as to the veracity of his exposition of the wonders of telephony as exemplified in the company's instrument—an incredulity that seems to have dogged his audiences down to to-day. This was coupled with obvious uncertainty as to whether they ought or ought not to tip the lecturer, "a question," he adds, "they either decided in the negative or never decided at all ; for I never got anything."

After this commercial experience "all attempts to earn an honest living" lapsed ; and

a period of utter failure to obtain any sort of encouragement, recognition, or literary employment followed, and lasted until 1885. His fortunes during this period were at their lowest point ; and when, in 1881, an attack of small-pox left him " unmarked, but an anti-vaccinationist for life," his affairs seemed desperate ; for the repeated refusals of publishers and editors to touch his work seemed to stamp him as a hopeless failure in journalism and literature ; and his perseverance in the face of the straitened resources of his family had all the air of infatuated and heartless selfishness. He was not sustained even by belief in himself ; for, as he declares, " I was profoundly unsatisfied with what I produced, and worked by mere instinct, like a beaver."

This is the period of which he treated later when he wrote that, "when nobody would pay a farthing for a stroke of my pen," he managed to mix with people who spent at least as much in a week as he did in a year. The reason was to be found in the fact that he had the ability, through the accidental lack of

better knowledge, to "play a simple pianoforte accompaniment at sight more congenially to a singer than most amateurs"; thereby gaining glimpses of a sphere of social life otherwise unattainable.

In a recent reflection on this impecunious period he says: "I was poor and (by day) shabby. I stood for my self-respect on the things I had: probity, ability, knowledge of art, laboriousness, and whatever else came cheaply to me. I could walk into Hampton Court Palace and the National Gallery (on free days) and enjoy Mantegna and Michelangelo, whilst millionaires were yawning miserably over inept gluttonies; I could suffer more by hearing a movement of Beethoven's Ninth Symphony taken at a wrong tempo than a duchess by losing a diamond necklace."

His literary career did not properly begin until nine years after his first arrival in London, when, in 1885, it was practically inaugurated by Mr. William Archer, who was instrumental in his being appointed to the reviewing staff of the *Pall Mall Gazette*, under

The Man

W. T. Stead ; and the same friend shortly afterwards helped him to the post of art critic to *The World*, under Edmund Yates. From that time he earned his living by his pen. The previous nine years, however, were not entirely devoid of recognition, as his own record of what he calls " three successes," in a letter to the present writer, will show. " Ernest Radford's brother George (the County Councillor) got me five pounds for writing an article for one of his clients about patent medicines—I suppose it was wanted for an advertisement of some sort, and have not the least idea what became of it. G. R. Sims accepted an article for a paper he started called *One and All*. I think it was about Christian names ; and the price was fifteen shillings. And a fellow-lodger of mine procured me the sum of five shillings for some verses to be appended to an engraving which some publisher had bought. I wrote them as a burlesque, and was so conscience-stricken when he took them seriously and paid for them, that I wrote him some serious verses for

another picture. They so disappointed him that he dropped me at once, and my career as a poet came to an end."

What pulled him through the period of apparent failure was dogged hard labour with his pen. From 1879 to 1883 he produced five novels. The story of these unfortunate works has been recounted in an inimitable way in the preface to *Cashel Byron's Profession*. "I recall these five remote products of my nonage," he writes, "as five heavy brown-paper parcels, which were always coming back to me from some publisher, and raising the very serious financial question of the sixpence to be paid to Messrs. Carter, Paterson, & Co., the carriers, for passing them on to the next publisher." There being no publishers at that time adventurous enough to issue these remarkable fictions, their author turned to other literary labours. Despised and rejected of publishers, the novels eventually became the incidentals of the literary output of a militant socialist.

The five novels of his "nonage" were

The Man

respectively entitled, No. 1, *Immaturity* (1879);
No. 2, *The Irrational Knot* (1880); No. 3,
Love Among the Artists (1881, interrupted by
the small-pox attack); No. 4, *Cashel Byron's
Profession* (1882); and No. 5, *An Unsocial
Socialist* (1883). Nos. 4 and 5 first sought a
public in the pages of the now extinct Socialist
magazine *To-Day*, and later on No. 4, *Cashel
Byron's Profession* (it was printed from the
stereotyped plates of *To-Day*), became his first
separately published volume. This "mis-
shapen shilling edition" was well reviewed by
Mr. William Archer and Mr. John M. Robertson, and it also won the admiration of Steven-
son. W. E. Henley wanted to have it dramatised. The *Saturday Review* declared it "the
novel of the age." Following such an exalted
cue, "the other papers hastily searched their
waste-paper baskets for it and reviewed it,
mostly rather disappointedly; and the public
preserved its composure and did not seem to
care." A revised shilling edition was placed
on the market by Messrs. Walter Scott,
and in 1901 the adventures of *Cashel Byron's*

Profession assumed finality in the prefaced and appendiced edition issued by Mr. Grant Richards, to which was added a dramatised version in blank verse entitled *The Admirable Bashville, or Constancy Unrewarded.*

The publication of No. 5 brought its author at least one asset. This was the acquaintance of William Morris, who, to the author's surprise, "had been reading the monthly instalments with a certain relish." Nos. 2 and 3 saw the light in another propagandist magazine, *Our Corner*, owned and edited by Mrs. Annie Besant. This excellent little monthly flourished in the year 1886, and had for contributors Charles Bradlaugh, John M. Robertson, Hypatia Bradlaugh Bonner, as well as Mrs. Besant and George Bernard Shaw, who, besides his novels, contributed the monthly article on Art. Here is his own description of the circumstances connected with the publication of novels No. 2 and No. 3 :—

"On the passing of *To-Day*, I became novelist in ordinary to a magazine called *Our*

The Man

Corner, edited by Mrs. Annie Besant. It had the singular habit of paying for its contributions, and was, I am afraid, to some extent a device of Mrs. Besant's for relieving necessitous young propagandists without wounding their pride by open almsgiving. She was an incorrigible benefactress, and probably revenged herself for my freely expressed scorn for this weakness by drawing on her private account to pay for my jejune novels. At last *Our Corner* went the way of all propagandist magazines, completing a second nonage novel and its own career at the same moment. This left me with only one unprinted masterpiece, my Opus 1, which had cost me an unconscionable quantity of paper, and was called, with merciless fitness, 'Immaturity.' Part of it had by this time been devoured by mice, though even they had not been able to finish it. To this day it has never escaped from its old brown-paper travelling suit."

The Irrational Knot was reissued in 1905 with a preface. These recent reissues have been partially of a protective nature, for some of

the novels in a mutilated form had been enjoying an illicit vogue in America. "The novels so long left for dead in the forlorn-hope magazines of the eighties, have arisen and begun to propagate themselves vigorously throughout the new world at the rate of a dollar and a half per copy, free of all royalty to the flattered author." This surely is one of the strangest histories of a novelist in literature. First there is the remarkable performance of a young man writing five novels before the age of thirty, which, in spite of their author's contempt for them, are full of passages which indicate remarkable powers of observation and a fresh and individual point of view, to say nothing of their distinctive literary qualities. Then come their fruitless journeyings round the publishers, culminating as padding for "the forlorn-hope magazines of the eighties." Here it might have been expected they would have lain in their obscure graves, but in spite of their author's wishes they were doomed to resurrection. "I was to find later on that a book is like a child," he says ; "it is easier to bring it

The Man

into the world than to control it when it is launched there. As long as I kept sending my novels to the publishers, they were as safe from publicity as they would have been in the fire, where I had better, perhaps, have put them. But when I flung them aside as failures, they almost instantly began to show signs of life."

It was towards the close of this period of novel-writing that he suddenly struck into that movement towards Socialism which was beginning to become conscious of itself at about the time of his arrival in London. Henry George first awakened his mind to the importance of Land Reform. This resulted in his joining the old Land Reform Union (now the English Land Restoration League), and later Karl Marx opened the way to Socialism. As early as 1879 he had taken his first step towards public life by joining a debating society called the Zeletical Society, a junior offshoot of the once famous Dialectical Society which had sprung, years before, out of the discussions raised by John Stuart Mill's essay

on Liberty. Among the members of the
Zeletical Society were Mr. Sydney Webb,
Mr. Emil Garcke, and Mr. J. G. Godard.
The friendship with Mr. Webb, which began
in this way, proved lasting and fruitful.
"Sydney Webb," he has said, "was of more
use to me than any other man I ever met, and
will be of more use to England than any
other man of his time." Shaw's first attempts
as a speaker were so nervous and wretched,
according to his own account, that he resolved
to make a speech in public every week for a
year ; and it was in this way that he acquired
the habit of haunting public meetings, which
led to his hearing Henry George speak on the
15th December, 1882, at the Memorial Hall
in Farringdon Street. George set him study-
ing economics for the first time ; and Karl
Marx's *Capital* completed his conversion to
Socialism. By that time he had, by practice
and perseverance, become a presentable speaker
and debater. He was one of the early members of the Fabian Society, which he joined in
September, 1884. He was elected to the

The Man

Society's Executive Committee in the following December, and has served on that body ever since.

His activity and energy at this time amount almost to genius. He helped to found and keep going the Hampstead Historic Club, a private circle of students of Marx and Proudhon, which eventually became the British Economic Association. He lectured and debated here, there, and everywhere, becoming by sheer hard work and multiplicity of experience not only an accomplished public speaker, both indoor and open-air, but one of the most efficient propagandists of his time. As he was novelist in ordinary to *Our Corner*, so he became pamphleteer in ordinary to the Fabian Society. He edited the *Fabian Essays in Socialism* in 1889, two of the essays and, of course, the preface being from his own pen. One of the lectures he had previously delivered on the 7th September, 1888, to the Economic Section of the British Association at Bath.

Besides drafting and otherwise aiding the literary and economic production of Fabian

Tracts, he wrote over his own name: *The Fabian Society : Its Early History* (this was first read as a paper at a conference of the London and Provincial Fabian societies at Essex Hall on the 6th February, 1892); the *Impossibilities of Anarchism*, 1893; *Fabianism and the Empire*, 1900; *Socialism for Millionaires*, 1901; and *Fabianism and the Fiscal Question*, 1904. These pamphlets stand out among the rest of the justly famous Fabian Tracts. They are all marked by that individual note of philosophic wit which has made the writings of Bernard Shaw so distinct a feature of modern letters. Besides the official publications of the Fabian Society, there are others associated with his Socialist activities. The verbatim report of the debate with Mr. G. W. Foote on the *Legal Eight Hours Question* at the Hall of Science on 14th and 15th January, 1891, was issued as a pamphlet in the same year, and in 1904 he issued the *Common Sense of Municipal Trading* on the eve of the London County Council election, when he stood as a Progressive candidate for South St. Pancras, and was defeated

The Man

owing to his frank admission of the good points in the then Government's Education Bill of 1902, upon which question the contest hinged. He however sat as vestryman and borough councillor for St. Pancras from 1897 to 1903; and though the reactionary party was in an overwhelming majority during all that period, and he was the unofficial leader of the Progressive Opposition, he was invariably elected to more than his share of the committees in which the real work of such bodies is done, as he was found, rather unexpectedly, to be a steady attendant and a level-headed man of business, patient of detail and administrative drudgery.

It was presumably the stern call of "the muse of daily bread" that determined his advent into journalism in the year of his coming to London. Between that year and 1879 he "did a little devilling at musical criticism," and there are hints in a published admission of the beginning of a "Passion Play in blank verse, with the mother of the hero represented as a termagant." But this

youthful ambition was not completed. For ten years he contributed to the Press weekly critical articles on music first, and then on the drama. These began on music in *The Star* in 1888–90 over the pseudonym *Corno di Bassetto*; and were continued in *The World* from 1890–4. Then came the famous *Saturday Review* dramatic criticisms from January, 1895, to May, 1898, which gave him a unique place among dramatic critics. A selection of these, entitled *Dramatic Opinions*, was issued in the spring of 1906, in two volumes, under the editorship of James Huneker. Besides his regular work for the weekly Press, there are several instances of departure from his beaten track; among these are two essays which must be reckoned among his more important works. The first is a letter contributed to the pages of Benjamin R. Tucker's paper *Liberty*[1] in refutation of Max Nordau's *Degeneration*; this fine piece of criticism is much more than an ordinary letter, it is a masterly essay nearly filling the whole issue of

[1] New York, July 27, 1895.

The Man

the paper. The second is *On Going to Church*, perhaps his finest essay from the point of view of pure literature, which appeared in the first number of *The Savoy* in January 1896. This period of journalism was one requiring great emphasis of personality, a faculty Bernard Shaw proved himself capable of supplying, for, after all, it was in the columns of the weekly Press that he first found himself.

The discovery was the result of his characteristic earnestness, coupled with the fact that he not only had something to say, but knew quite clearly what that something was, and that it was worthy of his pen. This made his essays things to give even the most hardened newspaper reader pause and make him either pleased or vexed. And in spite of that mordant humour which misled many, the few, at all events, recognised that behind this sprightly and trenchant journalism was a mind that, besides being earnest and painstaking, was fearless. Out of this work grew the G.B.S. not only of fact but of fiction : the one G.B.S. created for a public prod ; the other G.B.S.,

whom he considers the most successful of his fictions, is the G.B.S. whom wise men read, mark, learn, and inwardly digest. This ten years of journalism was, as he says, an apprenticeship which made him master of his own style.

There are two books belonging to the period—one, *The Quintessence of Ibsenism* (1891), coming at the beginning ; the other, *The Perfect Wagnerite* (1898), coming at the close— these form good examples of that consistency of thought and aim which characterises his career. Both exhibit that mingling of practical politics with the more abstract thought : a mind seeking a solution of its ideas in practical conduct. *The Quintessence of Ibsenism* was originally a Fabian lecture, and its genesis is explained in the preface.

"In the spring of 1890, the Fabian Society, finding itself at a loss for a course of lectures to occupy its summer meetings, was compelled to make shift with a series of papers put forward under the general heading *Socialism in Contemporary Literature*. The Fabian Essayists,

The Man

strongly pressed to do 'something or other,' for the most part shook their heads ; but in the end Sydney Olivier consented to 'take Zola' ; I consented to 'take Ibsen' ; and Hubert Bland undertook to read all the Socialist novels of the day, an enterprise the desperate failure of which resulted in the most amusing paper of the series. William Morris, asked to read a paper on himself, flatly declined, but gave us one on Gothic Architecture. Stepniak also came to the rescue with a lecture on modern Russian fiction ; and so the society tided over the summer without having to close its doors, but also without having added anything whatever to the general stock of information on Socialism in Contemporary Literature. After this I cannot claim that my paper on Ibsen, which was duly read at the St. James's Restaurant on the 18th July, 1890, under the presidency of Mrs. Annie Besant, and which was the first form of this little book, is an original work in the sense of being the result of a spontaneous internal impulse on my part."

This probably would have been the end of *The Quintessence of Ibsenism* had not the performance of *Rosmersholm*, *Ghosts*, and *Hedda Gabler* in London " started a frantic newspaper controversy" in which Bernard Shaw promptly realised that none of the disputants had ever been forced to make up their minds as to what Ibsen really meant. So with that desire to inform people which is a part of his nature, the old lecture was rewritten, and with additions was issued to the public in its present form. On the other hand, whilst actuated by the same public-spirited desire, *The Perfect Wagnerite* did not begin in Fabianism, but it took care to end there. It was issued in 1898 as a commentary on the *Nibelung's Ring*, and takes the form of an interpretation of Wagner's greatest work in the light of the revolutionary ideas of 1848, of which Wagner was an enthusiastic supporter. In the preface Shaw says :—

" All I pretend to do in this book is to impart the ideas which are most likely to be lacking in the conventional Englishman's equipment. I came by them myself much as

The Man

Wagner did, having learnt more about music than about anything else in my youth, and sown my political wild oats subsequently in the revolutionary school. This combination is not common in England ; and as I seem, so far, to be the only publicly articulate result of it, I venture to add my commentary to what has already been written by musicians who are no revolutionists, and revolutionists who are no musicians."

During these years of a literary activity which was considerably enhanced latterly by the writing and production of plays, Bernard Shaw found time to respond to the demands that are always made upon the time and ability of a capable revolutionary. This was to a considerable extent concentrated in the aims of the Fabian Society and its correlative bodies. But his skill as a debater and his sparkling facility as a public speaker opened up new possibilities for work of which organisers of Socialist clubs, and later, of any and every society that includes lectures in its activities, were not loth to make use. Shaw

reciprocated and gave them of that brilliant witty, and thought-provoking oratory, which was urged into fluency and confidence during his apprenticeship to the Socialist movement beneath the Reformer's Tree in Hyde Park, at many a meagre open-air meeting, and at innumerable hole-and-corner clubs all over London. Since these 'prentice days in London he has spoken all over the provinces to continually growing audiences.

He has a resonant but not by any means an orator's voice, rather the voice of a good conversationalist. In fact his platform eloquence is more akin to the extension of conversational periods into monologue than to ordinary oratory. As his writing lacks what is generally accepted as literary style or polish, so his speaking possesses none of the usual trappings of the platform. Yet the style is there—at least the only thing that is worthy the name of style is there—that is, the distinction given to things by contact with a commanding personality. His attitude towards his audience is that of one who is informing them as much

The Man

for their own good as because he is irritated at
their remaining in ignorance of the things
they ought to know : a knowledge of which
would in all probability make them more
agreeable to him. This would be an impossible attitude for a public speaker did he not
possess a sense of humour in addition to
religious or humanitarian fervour, and wit
as well as skill in applying a balm to the
wounded pride of his hearers. The attribute
of humour has never been denied him, and
when uttered as it is with a not too emphatic
brogue there is an additional charm to the
spoken words of this candid friend of the
people.

The latest literary phase of Shaw is that of
dramatist. As a maker of stage plays it has
been his lot to win at last something like fame ;
though, indeed, it is long ago since he lacked
what is greater than fame—the recognition of
his peers. His own story of his gravitation
from dramatic criticism to dramatic authorship
is suggestive of pecuniary necessity and a
desire to supply the necessary " new " play-

wright for the "new" theatre movement of the early nineties. Though this candid admission may be, and probably is, taken for a piece of bluff in the first instance and vain boast in the second, it is best to accept it at its face value. It is fully in keeping with the deliberation of Shaw's whole career. Weekly journalism he knew perfectly well could not be continued at a high level of sincerity for any length of time. It must inevitably, in the light of human capacity, become stale, used up, and ultimately fall back on empty repetitions and those vague generalities which adorn the pages of the contemporary commercial Press. This prospect was quite sufficient to force a man in earnest to look out for another means of livelihood, and the play, being in the line of his activities, naturally suggested itself. There was reason also for this in the fact that after the novel-writing period there was a futile attempt at dramatic authorship in collaboration with Mr. William Archer in 1885. The result of this partnership in creative enterprise was *nil*, so far as the

The Man

collaboration went, as may be gathered from this passage from the preface to Volume I of the *Plays: Pleasant and Unpleasant* :—

"Laying violent hands on his (Mr. Archer's) thoroughly planned scheme for a sympathetically romantic 'well-made play' of the type then in vogue, I perversely distorted it into a grotesquely realistic exposure of slum-landlordism, municipal jobbery, and the pecuniary and matrimonial ties between them and the pleasant people of 'independent' incomes who imagine that such sordid matters do not touch their own lives." The sequel was that Mr. Archer "promptly disowned" him. But two acts were written by the realistic party of the collaboration, to which a third was added in 1892, and the whole presented to the public at the Royalty Theatre by Mr. Grein under the title *Widowers' Houses*.

"The first performance," says its author, "was sufficiently exciting: the Socialists and Independents applauded me furiously on principle; the ordinary playgoing first-nighters hooted me frantically on the same ground; I,

being at the time in some practice as what is impolitely called a mob orator, made a speech before the curtain ; the newspapers discussed the play for a whole fortnight not only in the ordinary theatrical notices and criticisms, but in leading articles and letters ; finally the text of the play was published with an introduction by Mr. Grein, an amusing account by Mr. Archer of the original collaboration, and a long preface and several elaborate controversial appendices in the author's most energetically egotistical fighting style." So this proved his first play both in order of composition, performance, and publication. It was also the first number of the Independent Theatre's series of published plays, which included plays by Tolstoy and Maeterlinck.

The plays written between 1892 and 1896 were included in the two volumes published in 1898 under the title, *Plays: Pleasant and Unpleasant*. The first volume contained the *Unpleasant* plays, namely *Widowers' Houses: A Play; The Philanderer: A Topical Comedy;* and *Mrs. Warren's Profession: A Play.* The

The Man

Pleasant plays in Volume II were four in number, *Arms and the Man: A Comedy; Candida: A Mystery; The Man of Destiny: A Trifle;* and *You Never Can Tell: A Comedy.* All have been publicly performed except *Mrs. Warren's Profession.* The Philanderer only received nominal publicity in the first instance in a performance necessary to ensure the author's rights. This was due to the fact of its comedy parts being above the capacity of the Independent Theatre's company at the time it was written in 1893. It has since, and quite recently, had a successful "run" at the Royal Court Theatre and been placed in the repertoire of Messrs. Vedrenne & Barker. *Mrs. Warren's Profession* came under the ban of the Censor of Plays and was not performed until 1902, when it was presented privately by the Stage Society in the theatre of the New Lyric Club on the 5th and 6th of January. The occasion was celebrated by a re-issue of the play in a separate volume with a long prefatory "apology" from the author and excellent photographs of the players by Mr.

Frederick H. Evans. More recently (1905) *Mrs. Warren's Profession* set New York and the United States generally agog by its legal suppression (since rescinded), after two public performances, one in New Haven and the other in New York City. Performances were possible there because the law provides that no magisterial veto of a play can be exercised until after at least one performance.

Three Plays for Puritans, containing *The Devil's Disciple, Cæsar and Cleopatra,* and *Captain Brassbound's Conversion,* was published in 1901 ; in 1903 *Man and Superman* sought publicity as a volume with much additional matter in the form of prefaces and appendices, one of these last being *The Revolutionist's Handbook,* supposed to emanate from the pen of John Tanner, the anarchist hero of the play. It is in these prefaces and appendices with which all his volumes are re-issued that the philosophic genius of Bernard Shaw has become most expository, and his predilection for explaining himself has reached heights of witty and passionate exposition that

The Man

has made them unique in literature. In fact, the use of this method of exposition of the written drama is a discovery of first importance, and will no doubt become usual in the more earnest dramatic publications. For it makes it possible now for dramatists who, like Ibsen, have something to say apart from merely telling a pretty or thrilling story, which may be variously construed from the symbolic representations of the stage, to say definitely in the printed version of their work what actual idea they had in mind during its construction—a task which, apart from the amiable and popular desire for commercial success, would no doubt cause considerable difficulty to many of our native playwrights.

Man and Superman was issued before its public performance, which did not take place until the year 1905. In the same year at the Royal Court Theatre *John Bull's Other Island* (written originally for the Irish National Theatre), *How He Lied to Her Husband*, and *Major Barbara* were produced, and in 1906 *The Doctor's Dilemma*. Of these four the last

only has not yet appeared in book form. The three others appeared in June (1907) in a volume which contains, in addition to the plays, some of the best examples of the prefatory art of which he is a master. With the performance of *John Bull's Other Island* the public, or more properly speaking *a* public, has realised how enjoyable a drama of ideas can be when written by Shaw, and a consequent fashion has set in which demands as much Bernard Shaw as the proprietors of the Sloane Square Theatre can supply.

He did not marry until 1898, when in Miss Charlotte Frances Payne-Townshend he found a kindred spirit. Mrs. Bernard Shaw serves with him on the executive committee of the Fabian Society, and takes a keen and capable interest in his art and his many public activities. Although of late the number of his lectures to small societies has necessarily been curtailed, he is still a familiar figure at public Socialist meetings. He is as familiar, in fact, on the platform of ideas as his drama is in the theatre of ideas, and he always finds time, ful-

The Man

filling the adage that the busiest man has the most time to spare, to help voice the cause of progress, be it Socialism in England or Enfranchisement in Russia, or the less emphatic but none the less important aims of the numerous societies interested in the modern presentation of philosophy and art.

Still, even with this picture of steady energy in the service of ideas which are decidedly inimical to all that makes for the oppression of humanity—that same humanity has not enough common sense to see in him anything but a brilliant farceur. But here one must not be too hard on the ordinary folk who man the national ships ; for after all as has been said, the G.B.S. of the public mind is not of the public creation ; this feat must be laid at the door of G.B.S. himself. It was he who created the fascinating irritant. The G.B.S. of fiction was brought into being by the G.B.S. of fact. "I have advertised myself so well," he says, "that I find myself almost as legendary a person as the Flying Dutchman."

The non-legendary G.B.S. is, however, by

no means unfamiliar to Londoners in his corporeal state. In his earlier days in London Bernard Shaw was, as is well known, notable in matters of appearance; sandy-haired and Jaeger-clad, with a short beard that had never made acquaintance with a razor. But to-day he is more like other men to look upon in so far as his clothes, if not his beard, are of somewhat formal cut and cloth. His sandy hair, which is parted in the middle and brushed well back from a square forward brow, and his beard, which is longer than of yore, are toned down with grey. He is of the average height and easy in carriage; his head, which is remarkably square between the brows with a crown which depends towards the neck in a line unusually free from curve, is set well back, and his ears have a forward tilt. His eyebrows are at the mephisto-angle, and he has steady blue eyes. It is the head of a fighter who prefers a frontal attack. At the same time there is, in his general appearance, a hint of one who could strike comfortable attitudes and lounge had he the desire to do so; there

The Man

is again something about his immobile, yet alert head in strange contrast with his curiously mobile and expressive arms and hands. This is well brought out on the platform in moments of oratorical heat, when with head thrown back, hair and brows seeming to bristle, and eyes sparkling to match his peculiar eloquence, he stands quite still, but moves his hands and arms in a kind of gesticulating punctuation. Not, however, the swinging notes of exclamation which are the gesticulating stock-in-trade of the politician with the roaring oratorical manner, but movements of hand and wrist, and even elbow, which add the commas, semi-colons, full-stops, and interrogatory notes, to his irresistibly spoken sentences.

The personality of Bernard Shaw speaks through his appearance. To look at him one would immediately conclude that he cared little for what others thought of him, but much as to what he thought of himself. His pose is unconsciously deliberate and quite frank, and entirely free from superior reserve. He is an approachable man and he looks it.

And although he is free from the super-polish of the carefully-groomed city man, there is a well-ordered and easy neatness in his appearance which is innate rather than adopted. This absence of pose in one who is ostensibly on appreciative terms with himself is unexpected. But it is quite in keeping with his inner necessity for energetic self-expression coupled with a natural dislike of the merely decorative in life. His personal appearance is that of a man who stands for *something*, but that something is not formal ornament or fashion, even were it of his own creating. It is a form expressive of power—power to accomplish his own ends.

And one of the accomplishments of this personality is the creation of an intellectual conception of himself that holds a greater place in the contemporary mind than the reality, and one fears now that the reality would take less laying than its ghost. However, half a loaf is better than no bread at all, and as the G.B.S. of fiction is by no means so mythical as Mrs. Harris, we have cause to hope. The process of creation seems to have been along the

line of the exaggerated personalisation of all the more whimsical, humorous, and paradoxical traits in his character, with the salient omission of the steadying value of seriousness which is behind all but the hopelessly frivolous types. The creation of this figure out of the most conscious tendencies of a distinct personality was bound to be attractive, and the author was readily taken at his word. But he is now "getting a bit tiresome" even to his creator. "G.B.S.," he says, "gets on my nerves and bores me," adding with a suggestive reference to that seriously purposeful side of his character of which I have spoken, "except when he is working out something solid for me, or saying what I want said." So probably the public also will grow aweary of this facile G.B.S. and demand better acquaintance of the less entertaining but more satisfying personality behind the veil of amazing anti-climax and elusive wit.

The real Bernard Shaw is a fact. He is just one of those minds which must be grappled with before any proper conception of

modern thought is possible. His attitude towards society is a critical one, and his work stands for the conception of society minus the traditional and romantic glamour which is three parts of the average view of things. He is, in short, a realist with the courage of his convictions, which happen to be his own in this instance and not another's. This explains the parrot cry of originality which dogs his utterances like an evil spirit. "What the world calls originality" he says, "is only an unaccustomed method of tickling it." It is this unaccustomed tickling that is a by-product of Shaw's genius. He is not only a realist with the courage of his conviction, but, what is more rare, he is in his own existence an epitome of his opinions. These opinions, in short, are nothing more nor less than the philosophic deductions of his own personality. He deliberately exploits his personality for the benefit of humanity and the satisfaction of an abnormal desire for a seemliness in social life which, in his case, has begun at home.

He sees things from an aspect which might

be called traditionless, in so far as tradition is dominated by actuality. It has been explained by himself as an excess of normality of sight; a quickness of vision which must be so rare as to be almost abnormal. What is abnormal in his vision is the readiness with which the critical and perceptive faculties of the brain work together. His own record of a visit to an ophthalmic surgeon is worth noting here.

"He tested my eyesight one evening, and informed me that it was quite uninteresting to him because it was 'normal.' I naturally took this to mean that it was like everybody else's; but he rejected this construction as paradoxical, and hastened to explain to me that I was an exceptional and highly fortunate person optically, 'normal' sight conferring the power of seeing things accurately, and being enjoyed by only about ten per cent of the population, the remaining ninety per cent being abnormal. I immediately perceived the explanation of my want of success in fiction. My mind's eye, like my body's, was 'normal';

it saw things differently from other people's eyes, and saw them better."

This normality of sight he would no doubt extend to the description of his personal affairs, his daily round of social performances, his habits being of so simple an order as to make of him the 'odd man out' in society. Yet they have contributed more than anything towards that independence of expression which has made him a force in modern thought—a distinct personality. He early realised, as we have seen, the truth that freedom was largely determined by the things we can do without, a truth which, fully realised, makes comparative poverty, no less than the comforts that the swing of the pendulum may offer, less evil and destructive. "Simplicity is the last refuge of complexity," said Oscar Wilde; a paradox which is strangely true in the light of Bernard Shaw's description of his own simple life. "I cannot say that I have much experience of real poverty," he says, "quite the contrary. Before I could earn anything with my pen, I had a magnificent library in Bloomsbury, a priceless

The Man

picture gallery in Trafalgar Square, and another
at Hampton Court, without any servants to
look after or rent to pay. As to music, I
actually got paid later on for saturating myself
with the best of it from London to Bayreuth.
Nature and mankind are common property.
Friends! Lord bless me, my visiting list has
always been of an unpurchasable value and
exclusiveness. What could I have bought
with more than enough money to feed and
clothe me? Cigars? I don't smoke. Cham-
pagne? I don't drink. Thirty suits of
fashionable clothes? The people I most avoid
would ask me to dinner if I could be persuaded to wear such things. Horses?
They're dangerous. Carriages? They're
sedentary and tiresome. By this time I can
afford to sample them; but I buy nothing I
didn't buy before. Besides, I have an imagination. Ever since I can remember, I have
only had to go to bed and shut my eyes to be
and do whatever I pleased. What are the
trumpery Bond Street luxuries to me, George
Bernard Sardanapalus!" That is the person-

ality he has distilled into a philosophy and expressed in art.

It was largely this simple demand upon material things that made it possible for him to keep his art clean of mercenary temptations. It is the artificial needs created by the civilisation under which we live that are largely responsible for the prevalence of that scamping so obvious in the art work of to-day. The writer or painter, the musician or sculptor who desires to keep the ever-increasing pace of the luxurious middle class, must produce something that the rich will buy at a high price, or that the masses who are not rich will buy at a low price, but in such numbers as will make up the difference. Art is dependent for its reward upon the demands of these two classes. If such a reward is the demand of the artist then there is ample opportunity for realising it. On the other hand the artist who desires other reward than the satisfying of the superficial tastes, or deeper prejudices of the major portion of humanity, must have other means of subsistence or lessen his denominator.

The Man

Shaw lessened his denominator. This probably was no privation. His tastes were not the popular tastes. They were not tastes that would require the income of a Cabinet Minister to satisfy. He contained in his own composition almost all that most people have to seek and buy dearly elsewhere.

But apart from the exigencies of his circumstances Bernard Shaw's method of living has been largely, as might be deduced from the last quotation, the result of a kind of super-tastefulness. He is in reality an epicurean. His taste is distinctive and severe to fastidiousness. It is by nature peculiarly free from what is gross, and if at points it leans towards what is ascetic, this is entirely due to predilection. There is evidence of a selective ordering of his life, and in a way his habits remind one of the New Cyrenaicism of Pater. Like Marius the Epicurean he would seem to have condemned all in himself that had " not passed a long and liberal process of erasure," and his attitude towards society is a critical extension of this process to the things he considers socially blameworthy.

Bernard Shaw

At the same time the virility with which his criticism of society is imbued has its parallel in his personality. It is here that Shaw parts company with such a type as Marius. One never feels for a moment that his sensitiveness to what is ugly is neurotic, but rather that it results from a kind of nervous health; a robustness of feeling that rejects rather than fears what is offensive. His mind is no slave of the introspective habit. No sooner is he convinced of the practicability of an idea than he takes action. He is no brooder. This is why he becomes something rather than remaining a mere advocate of something. His mind responds readily to his feelings—in fact, his mind is the conscious instrument and interpreter of a rare and assertive taste.

He is neither so remote nor so reticent as Pater's exquisite hero, and there is a note of humour and abandonment in his utterance that would have made Marius shrink. "Lenten fare" with Shaw has by no means produced "lenten thought," and his sharpness of wit is bitter-sweet, savouring of his beloved fruits.

The Man

And although his tastes are so instinctive they are quite deliberate. One feels that he has taken pains to know what he wants. Indeed, this is a notable characteristic. As he did not shirk the drudgery incidental to his municipal experiences, neither does he delegate the spade-work of the ordinary channels of an author's days.

With the exquisite ordering of his life there goes along a magnanimity which will surprise those who know him only through the ironic Shawisms of the paragraphist. He has given himself freely. He has given of his best for years without reward. He has worked un-remittingly for a despised cause, and now that he has fame he does not alter his course. And although his word is bitter for the things he knows to be wrong, no one has been more generous in his estimation of the things he upholds—even when they are the products of a younger generation that may supplant the older, including himself. Bernard Shaw says " come in " to the Younger Generation knock-ing at the door. This magnanimity which

does not fear its own fame is closely related to a noticeable freedom from any tendency to condescension on his part, and he seems to be immune from those prevalent complaints of the artistic fraternity which express themselves in personal pique. He is not susceptible to petty offence, and he suffers fools with indifference, if not with gladness. He can take a blow with as much good humour as he can give one. He has none of that righteous indignation which is a very common form of self-defence, but in place of it we have his explanations—he does not defend himself, he explains himself.

His method of admonishing a lethargic public has not had any instantaneous good results. And the quality of his humour, as has been indicated, is probably the main cause of this, in addition, of course, to a corresponding lack of it in his readers. For the more he lashes these amiable folk the more they laugh—in fact, the extent of the public's amusement at Bernard Shaw is the extent of their missing the point.

The Man

But recently there is a marked change. Some of his utterances have struck home, and the gentlemen in the first-class compartment say this fellow is going too far, and reasoning from the recent success of the Vedrenne-Barker productions of his plays, argue that G.B.S. is overcome with his own importance and imagines he is privileged to say what he will, because they, forsooth, have condescended to laugh at what he has said. The humour of it (and the sadness of it also) is that Shaw never intended laughter to be final in the first instance, and in the second, the things that surprise them so much to-day are the selfsame things he has been saying for the past twenty years. If there is a fault it is in his public who have necessitated this reiteration. The G.B.S. of fiction ought to have been exploded long ago and his creator at work on the next creation. But let us hope that his philosophic hammer has at last tapped a vulnerable spot on John Bull's anatomy, and that that gentleman is now in the way of learning what discriminating students have known for years.

Bernard Shaw

It must also be borne in mind that the amused attitude of the public towards G. B. S. is reciprocated by himself, for Shaw has many of the traits of a laughing philosopher, although his laughter is what Meredith would call "the laughter of the mind—nearer a smile." He does not pretend to be amused, not even in the spirit of comedy, dear to the author of "Diana of the Crossways." His laughter is more in the nature of a whip—it stings while it pleases, but it is meant as a scourge. He sees life steadily and sees it whole with such pertinacity that he is overwrought by every inconsistency, and he laughs aloud when another might wail as Jeremiah did, or utter splendid wrath like Isaiah, or be imperturbably patient like Job. These are various methods—each in its way effective. But Bernard Shaw laughs at the ways of men with Aristophanes, with Rabelais, and with Heine—and he is none the less serious. A great deal of the mirth-provoking matter in his work is no laughing matter at all and was never meant to be; no more a laughing matter than the wisdom of

The Man

Keegan in *John Bull's Other Island* is insanity. "My way of joking," says Keegan, "is to tell the truth; it is the funniest joke in the world," and this might be Shaw speaking—and probably is.

Readers of the *Autocrat of the Breakfast Table* will remember a suggestive observation to the effect that until a man sees himself as others see him there must be at least six persons in every dialogue between two. "It is natural enough," the Autocrat adds, "that among the six there should be more or less confusion and misapprehension." Something like this happens between most original authors and their public, and when you get a multiple personality like the author of the *Three Plays for Puritans*, with his prefaces and appendices bristling with criticisms objectively and subjectively personal, haranguing a public which is hyper-self-conscious and almost invincibly dull, your complications are as likely as not to be highly diverting. And apart from the ordinary six persons of the traffic between author and public, there is the disturbing element in this

instance of the first contracting party creating other diversions than the conventional trinity in his own person. He must create a G.B.S., for instance, who with the other three, the explanatory, the critical, and the creative, has succeeded in making the confusion of personality worse confounded.

However, the discriminating, before alluded to, have learnt that Bernard Shaw's various mediums of expression are the interpretations of a philosophy as consistent as Euclid, yet so broad as not to exclude any endeavour for the extinction of suffering and for the common participation in the joy of life by the energy of a will that is conscious of itself and quick to respond to the deep purpose of life—"the being used for a purpose recognised by yourself as a mighty one; the being thoroughly worn out before you are thrown on the scrap heap; the being a force of Nature instead of a feverish selfish little clod of ailments and grievances complaining that the world will not devote itself to making you happy." With this aim in view he has become a modern

The Man

Socrates—doing for England by means of stage-play and essay, lecture and epistle, what Socrates did for ancient Athens by conversation and example. The same spirit of social welfare breathes through his utterances, making of him another gadfly stinging by his skilled use of words the lethargic members of the state into rightful action.

II

THE FABIAN

The vitality which places nourishment and children first, heaven and hell a somewhat remote second, and the health of society as an organic whole nowhere, may muddle successfully through the comparatively tribal stages of gregariousness; but in nineteenth-century nations and twentieth-century empires the determination of every man to be rich at all costs, and of every woman to be married at all costs, must, without a highly scientific social organisation, produce a ruinous development of poverty, celibacy, prostitution, infant mortality, adult degeneracy, and everything that wise men most dread. In short, there is no future for men, however brimming with crude vitality, who are neither intelligent nor politically educated enough to be Socialists. (*Man and Superman*. Preface, pp. xv–xvi, 1903.)

II

THE FABIAN

A BETTER comprehension of the attitude
of Bernard Shaw towards society is obtained after a correct understanding of his
position as a Fabian Socialist, for the main
issues of his practical politics are summed up
in those two words. Many of his books and
plays may suggest social reform, some of them
demand it more or less directly—but each of
his books is only propagandist in the strictly
Fabian sense. Many of the plays lend themselves to sociological deduction in the scientific
sense apart from, yet as a decided outcome of,
their deeper philosophy. *Widowers' Houses*, for
instance, suggests Housing Reform ; *Mrs.
Warren's Profession*, alteration of the conditions
under which women earn their living ; *Major
Barbara* suggests the failure of Charity, and

so on. If we except a few passages, it is only in the avowedly propagandist volumes and pamphlets that Bernard Shaw frankly advocates Socialism. He reproves his fellows for their indifference to the claims of Socialism, but anything in the nature of tub-thumping is quite absent from these books. The indirect Socialist criticism of the plays is a Fabian characteristic. It is a part of that subtle and effective propaganda in the development of which Bernard Shaw has taken a prominent part.

But when one speaks of Bernard Shaw the Fabian, one does not mean that it is possible to put him in a pigeon-hole with a lot of other similar political details ; indeed, he is a good example of the dissimilarity of the Fabian Society's units, whose similarity lies in the adoption of a central idea and an agreement as to the method of its enunciation. The margin for possible idiosyncrasy in the Fabian Society is a generous one, wide enough to admit that play of individuality which exists, as Shaw says, in the Executive Committee, where it is

inspiring to learn "no one of us is strong enough to impose his will on the rest, or weak enough to allow himself to be overridden." In this chapter, under the word Fabian, are grouped all those outward and visible signs of his criticism of life which express themselves in either social or political practice. For there is a distinction about his Fabianism, his whole personality being in the nature of propaganda ; it is in his clothing, at his table, in his talk, and in his art. He is not merely a complete revolutionary in his attitude towards civilisation, but he is a complete Fabian in the scope and variety of his remedies. So when we are confronted with ideas of dietetic reform and Jaeger clothing, with hatred of "Sport" and Vivisection, side by side with exhortations on Land Nationalisation, the Re-administration of Municipal Areas, and the breeding of Supermen, a reasonable computation will trace these themes to the radii of a circle whose centre is the Fabian idea.

The beginning of Bernard Shaw's Socialism was, as we have seen, the hearing of Henry

George at the Memorial Hall, Farringdon Street, during the famous Single Tax campaign in England in 1882, and his eyes were opened to the economic needs of modern times in the cause of which he has worked ever since. After hearing George, he read Karl Marx's *Das Kapital*, and these two completed that revolution in his ideas which resulted in Socialism. The evolution of this into the Fabian idea is best told in his own words. He says : " The importance of the economic basis dawned on me : I read Marx, and was exactly in the mood for his reduction of all the conflicts to the conflict of classes for economic mastery, of all social forms to the economic forms of production and exchange. But the real secret of Marx's fascination was his appeal to an un-named, unrecognised passion—a new passion —the passion of hatred in the more generous souls among the respectable and educated sections for the accursed middle-class institutions that had starved, thwarted, misled, and corrupted them from their cradles. Marx's *Capital* is not a treatise on Socialism ; it is

The Fabian

a jeremiad against the bourgeoisie, supported by such a mass of evidence and such a relentless Jewish genius for denunciation as had never been brought to bear before. It was supposed to be written for the working classes ; but the working-man respects the bourgeoisie, and wants to be a bourgeois ; Marx never got hold of him for a moment. It was the revolting sons of the bourgeoisie itself—Lassalle, Marx, Liebknecht, Morris, Hyndman, Bax, all, like myself, bourgeois crossed with squirearchy—that painted the flag red. Bakunin and Kropotkin, of the military and noble caste (like Napoleon), were our extreme left. The middle and upper classes are the revolutionary element in society ; the proletariat is the Conservative element, as Disraeli well knew. Hyndman and his Marxists, Bakunin and his Anarchists, would not accept this situation ; they persisted in believing that the proletariat was an irresistible mass of unawakened Felix Pyats and Ouidas. I did accept the situation, helped, perhaps, by my inherited instinct for anti-climax. I threw

Hyndman over, and got to work with Sydney Webb and the rest to place Socialism on a respectable bourgeois footing : hence Fabianism."

At this time Socialism in England was beginning to have a separate consciousness—it was, in fact, becoming self-conscious. Hitherto there had been no strict line of demarcation between Socialism and Anarchism, to say nothing of the niceties dividing Communism and Collectivism. The whole revolutionary thought of the period was a turbulent and uncertain chaos of Utopian dreams and crude economics, mixed up with morals as wild as they were exalted, and uttered with the flamboyant decorations of an emotionalism that looked upon the consummation of the Socialist state as a thing of a few years. England was at last genuinely affected by the energy of continental Socialism. The Chartism of forty years back was being re-born, not as Chartism, which had been more or less effectively absorbed by Radicalism, but as something as old, yet new to our limited capacities for the

absorption of new ideas. English Socialism of the early eighties was composed of little more than the Communist Manifesto of Marx and Engels, which was first issued in 1847. The atmosphere, however, was quick with new hope, and a group of men of imagination and ability was attracted to the movement. Among these were H. M. Hyndman, William Morris, Belfort Bax, Herbert Burrows, H. H. Champion, John Burns, J. L. Joynes, H. Quelch, who, with Annie Besant, Sydney Webb, and Bernard Shaw, were the founders of English Socialism. They gave the insurrectionary communism of the Continent not merely a local habitation and a name in our midst, but transformed its externals so as to appeal the less shockingly to the traditional susceptibilities of our insular prejudices. They succeeded in turning their somewhat nebulous material into a moral and political machine of surprising and incalculable power.

The Fabian Society was the outcome of the natural conflict of ideas and methods of those early days of Socialist organisation. Hitherto

the constructive idea had received little attention; the Fabians conceived the policy of turning the stream of Socialist thought into the ordinary channels of our constitutional methods, and, instead of eternally preaching a doctrine from the house-tops, giving the machinery of legislation a practical collectivist bias. But this idea was by no means so clear as it eventually became when the Fabians were the first heretics to the "all or nothing" Socialism of 1883.

The actual formation of the Fabian Society came about as the outcome of a break, not so much with revolutionary Socialism, as with a kind of transcendental Individualism. This was introduced into England by Thomas Davidson, brother of Morrison Davidson, who had spent some time in Italy, where he came under the influence of the ethical philosophy of Rosmini, an influence which bore fruit in the form of the Fellowship of the New Life, a society for the propagation of ideal ethics, formed by Davidson in London. Meetings were held in his rooms at Chelsea

from 1881 to 1883, and a periodical called *Seedtime*, which lived for eight years, was issued. The need for larger accommodation caused the Fellowship to move its quarters to the rooms of Edward R. Pease, one of its members, at 17 Osnaburgh Street, Regent's Park. These rooms were destined to see the birth of the Fabian Society. The Davidson process, which Shaw describes as "the peaceful regeneration of the race by the cultivation of perfection of individual character," was found wanting by the more Socialist members of the Fellowship, and they agreed to separate. Those who left the Fellowship then were the first Fabians. Among those who were present at the meeting which decided to form a society whose aim should be the dissemination of ideas towards the regeneration of humanity by the capture of the legislative machinery of the state, and its administration for the common good, were Frank Podmore, Edward R. Pease, Havelock Ellis, Percival Chubb, Dr. Burns Gibson, H. H. Champion, William Clarke, Hubert Bland, Rev. G. W. Allen, and W. J. Jupp.

The first Fabian secretary was F. Keddell, a post occupied by him until 1885, when he was succeeded by Edward R. Pease. The secretaryship of the society has been in his able hands continuously since 1890; before this date there was a break of a year or so, owing to unavoidable absence from London, when Sydney Olivier (now Sir Sydney Olivier, K.C.M.G., Governor of Jamaica) acted in his place. The chief conspirator in the formation of the Fabian Society seems to have been Mr. Frank Podmore, who suggested the name "Fabian," after Fabius Cunctator, the Roman Consul, whose memory is chiefly preserved in the record of the success that followed his adoption of devious and prudential tactics in the art of war, and he invented the appropriate quotation which appeared in inverted commas on the title cover of the earlier Fabian Tracts :—

"For the right moment you must wait, as Fabius did most patiently when warring against Hannibal, though many censured his delays ; but when the time comes you must

strike hard, as Fabius did, or your waiting will be in vain, and pointless."

Gatherings were continued in the rooms of Mr. Pease, and the actual meeting, when the Fabians became established as a society, was held on January 4th, 1884. Bernard Shaw did not join until some eight months later; he was elected to membership on September 5th of the same year. He was on the point of joining the Democratic Federation when, he says, "guided by no discoverable difference in program or principles, but solely by an instinctive feeling that the Fabian and not the Federation would attract the men of my own bias and intellectual habits who were then ripening for the work that lay before us," he thereupon joined the organisation, of which he is still a member. It is interesting to note that immediately upon joining the society he became an active worker, suggesting lines of action, and writing tracts. Of these, Fabian Tracts Nos. 2 and 3, which are no longer issued, were his work, although much altered by the committee. They were called, *A Manifesto*

(1884), and *To Provident Landlords and Capitalists : A Suggestion and a Warning* (1885).

There was a specific Fabianism, however, though at this time it was in a latent state ; the very choice of name and the fact that it attracted men of a certain type of mind indicates some governing idea apart from and deeper than that of class distinction, which was one of the more obvious differences between the new and the older organisations. The League and the Federation, although led by members of the middle class, were always proletarian in aim and constitution, whereas the Fabian Society, though open to all classes, was of a decided bourgeois bias in both rank and file. Later this social difference made propaganda by means of constitutional opportunism and permeation a hopeful line of action. At first the Fabian Society was in reality a body of students whose one aim was the effective application of the collectivist idea to present affairs, and it was not until later in its career that permeation became a conscious factor in the science of theoretic and applied sociology.

The Fabian

Revolution by constitutional means is a fundamental Fabian idea. The society has never encouraged detached revolutionism, any more than it has advocated or condoned insurrectionism; in fact, Fabians have always been convinced that Socialism would be brought about without the Socialist detaching himself in any way from the normal course of English life. Bernard Shaw has always upheld this idea. It is evident in his invariable advice to the ardent young Socialist who wishes to do something for the cause. "Become efficient at your own particular trade or profession," he says, "and then tell every one you are a Socialist."

An important characteristic of the Society is the fact that whilst numbering among its members many of the most able sociologists living, it is still a society of students in the sense that it recognises the constant need for the re-statement of its ideas in the light of changing social conditions. This means that it not only seeks by devious ways to have its ideas put into force, but that it seeks to discover and

institute new sociological needs and tendencies, and its more active members fall roughly into two classes—the men of ideas, imaginative, philosophical, and scientific, like H. G. Wells and Bernard Shaw, Sydney Webb and Edward R. Pease ; and the practical men, organisers, members of Parliament, and municipal councillors, and all those members who do social service up and down the land.

But in certain instances these two classes are united in the same individual. This is conspicuously so in the case of Sydney Webb (and in this reference one must not forget Mrs. Sydney Webb, the brilliant partner of his social work), who unites the duties of London County Councillor and general practical adviser to all organisations associated with labour and industry, with an almost incredible power of painstaking research into the origin and nature of industrialism and the genesis and history of local government. And in Bernard Shaw we have another example of this combination ; but here it is with the philosophic and the practical, which last had ample play in his six

The Fabian

years' service as Vestryman and Borough Councillor of St. Pancras.

The Socialism of the Fabian Society in the past has been economic. Its aim is the re-organisation of Society on a basis that is free from the limitations imposed upon it by the private ownership of land and industrial capital, and it works towards the vesting of these in the community for the general benefit. More recently, however, the Society has admitted the philosophic aspects into its curriculum, and by means of a Fabian Arts Group, over the initial meeting of which Bernard Shaw presided, it is extending its usefulness by the study of the relations of art and philosophy to Socialism.[1]

[1] Quite recently the Fabian Society was urged to reconsider its basis, and to devise ways and means for extending its usefulness. The leader of what became a reform movement within the Society, was H. G. Wells. He was instrumental in having a special committee appointed to consider the present condition and future work of the Society. This committee eventually issued a report, to which the Executive Committee made a reply. A series of debates extending over many meetings followed, in which H. G. Wells and Bernard Shaw found themselves protagonists of opposing camps. Shaw was elected the spokesman of the "Old Gang" and how he acquitted himself is notable Fabian

Bernard Shaw

Bernard Shaw's contribution to the economic aim of the Society has been as exponent rather than as innovator, but his exposition of Socialistic ideas is so distinct as to be in the nature of creation. Ruskin was the first to humanise political economy, to turn it from a dismal into a joyful science; Bernard Shaw has gone a step further by making it appeal to common sense in a manner not only attractive but absolutely amusing. It is not a matter of popularising, as Robert Blatchford does, by graphic and sincere exposition in simple words addressed to the man in the street, but a witty, logical, and provocative appeal to the common sense and personal interest of all who have the latent elements of thought. It is in effect political economy in terms of inspired common sense—inspired from both practical, philosophical, and imaginative sources.

History, specially memorable to those who heard his magnificent fighting speech at Exeter Hall on 14 December, 1906. But although Wells was out-manœuvered in the debate on the Report of the Special Committee and the Reply of the Executive, the spirit of reform inaugurated by him dominates the Society and is already creating far-reaching activities.

The Fabian

This might be expected in a play with a purpose, though it is not always to be relied upon even there. But one does not usually anticipate a laugh in the works of the followers of the science of Adam Smith, John Stuart Mill, and Karl Marx. The effect of this hilarity of thought, which in some ways is a Fabian characteristic, has been similar to what Shaw himself records of the Society. "It was at this period," he says, referring to a stage in its growth, "that we contracted the invaluable habit of freely laughing at ourselves which has always distinguished us, and which has saved us from becoming hampered by the gushing enthusiasts who mistake their own emotions for public movements. From the first such people fled after one glance at us, declaring that we were not serious."

But this humoursome peculiarity has not always the advantage, for whilst ensuring the favour and support of those who are the fortunate possessors of a sense of humour plus a seriousness of thought and aim, it alienates not only those who "mistake their own

emotions for public movements" who, in reference to an author, are his sentimental parasites, but those more useful dull persons who are none the less earnest and in some instances even able in purpose. Many of these by reason of this shortage of humour are forced into the numerous band of duffers who see nothing in Shaw's work but a profusion of brilliant paradoxes that mean nothing and lead nowhere. But, after all, it does not need a sense of humour so much as a sense of honesty to realise the opposite to this conclusion, and that even the most whimsical utterance in the plays, read in the light of his Fabian essays, not to mention his philosophy, leads irresistibly to a conclusion decidedly the opposite of nowhere and nothing.

His two most remarkable contributions to both Fabianism and his own particular method of enunciating economics from the Socialist point of view, and as special propagandist efforts, are *Socialism for Millionaires*, first published in the *Contemporary Review* of February, 1896, and afterwards (1901) as Fabian Tract

The Fabian

No. 107; and *The Common Sense of Municipal Trading*, issued on the eve of the L.C.C. election in 1904. In each we have, with greater certainty than in any other of his actual Fabian essays, that whimsical and arresting humour applied to a purely matter-of-fact and common-sense view of modern social problems, with just that hint of a deeper philosophy behind, which raises even the most trivial and aggravating of his pronouncements from mediocrity.

The re-issue of *Socialism for Millionaires* was due to the fact of what he calls the "Millionaire Movement," which is the outcome of the "Substitution of Combination for Competition as the Principle of Capitalism," having produced "a new crop of individual fortunes so monstrous as to make their possessors publicly ridiculous." This had recently culminated in the expressed opinion of Mr. Andrew Carnegie that no man should die rich. The essay was therefore republished with Shavian benevolence as a guide to the voluntary expropriation of the absurd fortunes of this "millionaire class, a small but

growing one, into which any of us may be thrown to-morrow by the accidents of commerce." It sets forward the economics of the distribution of private wealth, and it is the first contribution to this class of sociology. There is incalculable harm done by well-intentioned plutocrats who "unload" their unearned increment unscientifically, and Shaw shows how, keeping one eye on science and the other on common sense, the greatest good can be done to society by even those who have been instruments of the greatest harm. The method is scientific in so far as it is applied in deference to certain known laws of social life and in reference to an organic conception of society as a whole. The folly of excessive incomes is contrasted with the possibilities of the income that never exceeds the bounds of practical and wise expenditure. "A man with an income of twenty-five pounds a year can multiply his comfort beyond all calculation by doubling his income. A man with fifty pounds a year can at least quadruple his comfort by doubling his

income. Probably up to even two hundred and fifty pounds a year doubled income means doubled comfort. After that the increment of comfort grows less in proportion to the increment of income until a point is reached at which the victim is satiated and even surfeited with everything that money can procure." This conclusion is undoubtedly true, as some of us can testify—at all events, up to the second and third doublings. As to what occurs in the increasing burden of income, we can only surmise by an act of the imagination, which, after all, should be as useful in sociology as in art. But Bernard Shaw does not trust us in this respect ; he supplies us, in a characteristic and whimsically true passage, with a picture of the incongruousness of the over-rich :

" What can the wretched millionaire do that needs a million ? Does he want a fleet of yachts, a Rotten Row full of carriages, an army of servants, a whole city of town houses, or a continent for a game preserve ? Can he attend more than one theatre in one evening,

or wear more than one suit at a time, or digest more meals than his butler? Is it a luxury to have more money to take care of, more begging-letters to read, and to be cut off from those delicious Alnaschar dreams in which the poor man, sitting down to consider what he will do in the always possible event of some unknown relative leaving him a fortune, forgets his privation? And yet there is no sympathy for this hidden sorrow of plutocracy. The poor alone are pitied. Societies spring up in all directions to relieve all sorts of comparatively happy people, from discharged prisoners in the first rapture of their regained liberty to children revelling in the luxury of an unlimited appetite; but no hand is stretched out to the millionaire, except to beg."

The negative rules for millionaires are: (1) Don't leave more than enough for a fair start in life to your children. (2) Don't give alms. Providing for families and giving alms are one and the same thing. "From the point of view of society, it does not matter a straw whether the person relieved of the necessity of

working for his living by a millionaire's bounty,
be his son, his daughter's husband, or merely
a casual beggar." This is, of course, a simple
law of economics that no society but one profoundly indifferent to such things would fail to
have put in practice. Any arrangement of
capital that makes it possible to increase the
power of consumption whilst either reducing
that of production or leaving it *in statu quo*
must ultimately act injuriously on the society.
As to the negation of almsgiving, had we
not examples of the entire failure of charitable
organisations to do anything more than reduce poverty in one place while its augmenta-
tion went on in another ? Sisyphus-like they
rolled their poverty boulder to the hill-top of
charity only to have it perpetually rolled
down again by natural economic laws ; or, in
other words, they found that the increase of
their charitable endeavour was parallel with an
increase in poor-law returns, unemployment,
pauperism, starvation, physical decay, and
social degeneration. In this essay Shaw shows
how absurd it is to "help" beggars. As a

matter of fact, the genuine beggar cannot be helped without danger to the social system; he points out rightly that this class is different from "the deserving poor." They are "people who have discovered that it is possible to live by simply impudently asking for what they want until they get it," and true almsgiving is inseparably linked with this class, which is just as parasitic as the idle rich—the folk who live on rent and dividends.

The whole art of millionaire unloading is contained in this rule: "The millionaire is never to do anything for the public, any more than for an individual, that the public will do (because it must) for itself without his intervention." This, of course, would rule out of countenance such gigantic schemes of library distribution as those practised by Mr. Carnegie, although the matter is here compromised by non-endowment and the insistence on rate support of the library presented by the millionaire. However, this does not place Mr. Carnegie's munificence on a properly progressive basis, for apart from the fact that it

The Fabian

stimulates an altogether demoralising spirit of importunity on the part of the privately minded members of our municipal councils, it destroys the possibility of citizenship that should aim at communal independence—especially in cases such as this where the statutes make provision for public libraries. Those who want books should buy them either collectively through the rates or privately—they should not beg, even from a millionaire.

So it will be seen that both the methods adopted by Mr. Carnegie and the late Cecil Rhodes, whilst sound in their recognition of the principle that it is immoral for a man either to die rich or bequeath his wealth at the instigation of the accidents of consanguinity, are equally unsound in aiding institutions that in one instance (libraries) are empowered by the state to help themselves, and in the other (colleges) ought to have that power from the state by natural right. The principle to be established is that charity is the greatest hindrance to the perfection of the state machine.

Bernard Shaw would welcome any financial

aid for the purpose, not of supplanting public machinery, but for setting public machinery in motion ; "it is the struggles of society to adapt itself to the new conditions which every decade of modern industrial development springs on us that need help." And any club or society that devotes itself to aiding the larger social organism towards these new conditions is worthy of help—any society that is in the nature of a Vigilance Committee such as the National Society for the Prevention of Cruelty to Children, the Commons Preservation Society, or, in his own words, "any propagandist society which knows how to handle money intelligently and which is making a contribution to current thought, whether Christian or Pagan, Liberal or Conservative, Socialist or Individualist, scientific or humanitarian, physical or metaphysical."

The concluding formula of this suggestive tract is, "Never give the people anything they want, give them something they ought to want and don't." There is no real excuse for millionaires who have read this tract—and for

the financially incumbrous it is a revelation in the economics of rent and interest and the public idea in relation to wealth, apart from its excellence as an essay in the wisdom of spending.

In the *Common Sense of Municipal Trading*, Bernard Shaw has presented a view of this important question, which is not over-stated in the title. The opponents of the recent municipal awakening, opponents be it noted generally drawn from the wealthy class associated with finance, trusts, and limited companies, and the immediate dependents and parasites of this class, have so bewildered an unthinking public with cleverly manipulated figures and industriously perverted facts, that that large and long-suffering body might almost be forgiven for acting against its interests and voting for the anti-municipal nominees. Therefore, a statement of the common sense of the question had become an urgent necessity ; and were the public repute for this article not a myth it would read this book with a peculiarly appreciative

relish. It is a statement of the case for municipal trading not in terms of figures and statistics, but in terms of life, for, he says with irrefutable truth, "the balance-sheet of a city's welfare cannot be stated in figures. Counters of a much more spiritual kind are needed, and some imagination and conscience to add them up as well." The treatise is not alone the outcome of theories, but of Bernard Shaw's six years' practical experience in the committee rooms of St. Pancras Vestry and Borough Council, so that even the most violent advocates of the practical may not read in vain.

There is no doubt that it is to the municipalities we must now turn for the affairs of the land that have a more intimate bearing upon our daily lives. The Central Parliament at Westminster must inevitably become more and more the director and arbiter of imperial circumstance clustered around by numerous Local Parliaments, growing in size rather than numbers, who will look to Westminster with a perpetual demand for fuller powers. The citizens who know their own business, who

are not entirely tradition bound, are those
who know this and work to realise it. They
have realised, as Bernard Shaw has, that the
great parliamentary battle of the near future
is to be between the pros and cons of what is
miscalled municipal trading—for the thing
that is meant by these words is not, properly
speaking, trading at all. It is service, public
service, the organisation and administration
of the people's affairs, so as to reduce waste
to a minimum, and by giving a wide margin of
convenience and health to make the maximum
of public growth possible.

It is the communalisation of utility and
ability that is involved in the question of
municipal service, and Shaw says without exaggeration that "it is conceivable by a sensible
man that the political struggle over it may
come nearer to a civil war than any issue
raised in England since the Reform Bill of
1832." He adds that "it will certainly not
be decided by argument alone. Private property
will not yield its most fertile provinces to the
logic of Socialism; nor will the sweated labour,

or the rack-rented and rack-rated City shop-keeper or professional man refrain, on abstract Individualist grounds, from an obvious way of lightening his burden." Perhaps here, however, whilst not supposing for a moment that the great monopolies in private property can be expropriated by entirely peaceful means, the growth of municipal administration may be continued by the necessity created out of its own impetus.

For instance, the social system is so knit together, in spite of the jarring sectarianism of competitive commerce, that any one private field of public exploitation can never become a machine of public service without implicating in numerous ways all its associated concerns. Again, the necessity of national defence makes a state-owned navy necessary, and the coaling of that navy suggests state-owned mines. In the case of private combinations, whose aim is the eradication of the waste of competition, they begin by manufacturing, say, soap, and end by making all the accessories of the manu-facture and distribution of soap, as well as

spreading into fresh industries by the utilisa-
tion of by-products and the accumulation of
profits, such as, in the former case, glycerine,
which in a small soap concern would be dele-
gated to a glycerine factor or allowed to run
to waste. Your soap-maker not only becomes
his own printer, box-maker, ship-owner, car-
rier, etc., but the centralisation of his concern
makes him town-owner, as at Port Sunlight,
where Messrs. Lever Bros. have built a model
village for the habitation of their workers.
So in this way the "peaceful penetration" of
the sacred realm of Private Property will be
continued for many years to come. It will
grow like a snowball, making a larger and
accumulating service with each revolution.

The impression left after reading *The Common
Sense of Municipal Trading* is not the acquies-
cent wonder experienced after an excursion
into the realms of the Utopists, but of amaze-
ment at the possible existence, which one begins
to doubt, of any opponents of municipalisa-
tion. There is a sweet reasonableness about it
all, an irresistible logic that should convince

even those who have something to lose by the idea of municipal service being pushed to its logical conclusion, namely, the rich. Whilst not lacking in brightness there are fewer tread-on-the-tail-of-my-coat Shawisms in this book than in his others, yet there are many instances of that truth of paradox which only one who is not standing on his head to attract attention could command. The first sentence in the following extract is paradoxical enough in the light of public opinion, but in the economic light that follows it assumes an air of common sense worthy of its cause.

"The truth about private enterprise is that it is not enterprising enough for modern public needs. It will not start a new system until it is forced to scrap the old one. And the reason—one that no profusion of technical education will wholly remove—is that only a fraction of the public benefit of industrial enterprise is commercially appropriable by it. It will not risk colossal capitals, with the certainty that it must do enormous service to the public and create a prodigious unearned incre-

ment for the ground landlords before it can touch a farthing dividend; and therefore, however crying the public need may be, if the municipalities will not move in the matter, nothing is done until millionaires begin to loathe this superfluity and become restless as to its investment; until railways are promoted merely to buy tubes from Steel Trusts, and monster hotels floated, after the usual three liquidations, to buy tables and carpets from furniture companies. And even then what is done is only enough to show that it should have been done fifty years sooner, and might even have been done commercially but for the fatal, though inevitable, commercial habit of mind which must consider only the dividend which it can grasp and not the social benefit that it must share with its neighbours."

The direct purpose of the book is to induce the public to see that it would be wiser for them to use all the channels of social benefit for social rather than private, for communal rather than commercial ends. It should open the eyes of the people who read the newspapers

to the absurdity of calling expenditure on municipal services such as gas, water, tramways, and other social benefits, municipal debt. These things are not debts, but the reverse ; the only real municipal debts are degradation of life and limitation of the healthy aspirations of the human soul to worthy endeavour. These worst debts of all are forced upon the municipality by the very individuals who prate most of municipal indebtedness. The opponents of organised labour find a margin of surplus labour a constant deterrent to the pursuit of higher wages and grow wealthy on casual labour that must by its very nature degenerate into rate-subsidised human wrecks. For, says Shaw : " No human being, however solid his character and careful his training, can loaf at the street corner waiting to be picked up for a chance job without becoming more or less of a vagabond." It is the creators of this degenerate type of humanity who cause the high rates which they use as a bogey to scare municipalisers. The poor rate is largely a levy imposed upon the majority of the

citizens in support of the veterans of industry who are derelict because of the dividends they have helped to make having gone into other pockets than their own.

Shaw has a profound grip of the economics of drudgery and all those mean and sordid things that are so evident in our cities. He does not speak in this book with the heat of an enraged prophet, he is no Isaiah, not even a Lassalle ; he speaks rather as one who is out of patience with the mess of modern commerce and with something bordering on contempt for the people—workers as well as capitalists—who uphold it. He would not shatter it to bits and then remould it nearer to his heart's desire, but he would remould it nearer to his heart's desire along the line of a sane and common-sense curve of social endeavour.

But Shaw is not a Utopist in the sense of one having a cut-and-dried Socialistic state ready to supplant the present order of affairs. He has not even interpreted the Socialist idea in terms of imaginative science as H. G. Wells has done in *A Modern Utopia*. In fact, he has not

gone so far in speculative sociology as Wells did in *Mankind in the Making;* and at one time, at least, he was indifferent to such imaginings. In December, 1896, he was announced to lecture at Kelmscott House, Hammersmith, on "What Socialism will be like," and the following passage from the report of his opening remarks will bear this out :—

"My lecture will be very short. It consists of three words—*I don't know*. Having delivered it, by way of opening a discussion, I will proceed to make a few remarks. The first thing that strikes one in discussing the matter with a Socialist—if you have a critical habit of mind, as I have, professionally—is the superstitious resemblance of the notion your ordinary Socialist has of what Socialism will be like to the good old idea of what heaven will be like ! If you suggest that under Socialism anybody will pay rent or receive wages, your ideal Socialist jumps on you. If I venture to suggest that such questions as who shall be allowed to live on Richmond Hill, under Socialism, will have to be settled

The Fabian

much as it is to-day, by seeing who will pay
most to live there, such an eminent and en-
lightened Socialist as Mr. Hyndman immediately loses his temper, and retorts that that is
a disgusting middle-class idea." [1]

Although there is a decided negation of
idealist Utopianism here, Shaw would probably take more seriously the Utopian studies
of H. G. Wells, which were, of course, unknown in 1896. At the same time, there is
evidence on his sociological as well as his
philosophical side of a strong objection to any
elaborate preconceptions of either states or persons. His idea of Socialism is not of a
definite state, but of a whole range of tendencies towards the reshaping of the social
order at the dictation of certain feelings and a
certain line of thought, which develops as it
proceeds. It may by the tentative nature of
its actions force what is called progress to-day
into an undreamed-of line of action to-morrow.
He would take circumstances as he finds them,
applying what remedies are known, and awaiting

[1] *The Labour Leader*, 19th December, 1896.

the resulting circumstance before deciding the next step.

At the same time, he is not without ideas as to what might be the possible development of, say, the wage system, or what will stimulate initiative and govern distribution under conditions wherein each unit is assured of the minimum of material necessaries. But even here he is free from any of the usual superstitions of the idealist. His Socialism is always too much in the company of practical politics to become a Shibboleth. This has been the cause of as much misunderstanding of his aims among Socialists as among the general public and the dramatic critics. So that the uninitiated are delighted to have their imprecations heartily corroborated by the very folks whom they expected to agree with him. But your orthodox Socialist does not take his Shaw any more seriously than your orthodox Conservative does. Shaw is a heretic, for instance, among Socialists who still uphold the Marxian Theory of Value, and the Referendum. And his views on the innumerable details of pro-

cedure and tactics, and in reference to what romantic tradition has already clustered around the Socialist movement, are usually provocative of controversy.

His practical attitude is most allied to that of his friend Sydney Webb, who is undoubtedly the best-informed of modern men on all questions relating to Industrialism—its cause and cure—and Local Government. The influences of this sociologist's calm and patient research into the various social defects of the day and of his sane and practical conclusions for reform are traceable throughout Bernard Shaw's Socialism, and there is little doubt that when the history of the Fabian Society is written it will be found that the chief instigators of its policy and tactics were these two. It was this rare combination of practical ability with science and wit, philosophy and imagination, that must have gone a long way towards fostering the enthusiastic collaboration which has been conspicuous in the life of the Society.

To the practical science of Sydney Webb, Bernard Shaw has added his own philosophy,

which, applied to politics, takes the form of a denunciation of the privately-minded temperament as against the social consciousness of the individual. His main idea is so to affect the social germ in the human constitution as to urge it into an endeavour against all impediments to its full development. One of his strongest terms of contempt is that of "hopelessly private person"—that numerous he who is quite content to value everything and sacrifice everything to personal vanity and greed. It is such content as this he would ruffle, not so much by moving the private persons to individual reformation as by creating a sufficient number of socially conscious beings to bring external pressure to bear on the others. He has little faith in the physician-heal-thyself moralists, although he would recognise the necessity for a fair average of capacity in the rank and file and of ability at the head. "It was easy," he says, "for Ruskin to lay down the rule of dying rather than doing unjustly; but death is a plain thing; justice a very obscure thing." That is why Shaw works for

The Fabian

the recognition of the utility of a properly
organised band of social experts whose business
it is to seize the political power of the country
and to use it for the adjustment of the social
balance, and to create a broad margin of
freedom based upon a social minimum established by the State instead of at the dictation
of the exigencies of property. It is the
arranging of a pitched battle between two
armies—one of Private Capital, the party
of social stagnation, and the other of Communal ideas, the party of social growth.

Two factions at least exist in every state
though their external demands change, and
their fight under democracy is for the posses-
sion of the majority before they can put their
ideas into force. To-day the conflicting forces
are capital and labour and the remedial ideas,
individualism and collectivism. Bernard Shaw
in ranging himself on the side of the collectivist does so because he recognises in the
state established by the individualist nothing
but human chaos—a social mess ; a condition
that can only be altered by administration of

the machinery of legislation in such a way as gradually to supplant the individualist by the collectivist regime, and not by the method "of those foolish misers of personal righteousness who think they can dispose of social problems by bidding reformers of society reform themselves first."

Socialist though he is, he does not hold to any views that would give the democracy complete control of its affairs. He recognises the fundamental inequality of the human egos whilst denying the necessity for economic inequality. Democracy he calls "the last refuge of cheap misgovernment," and he can by no stretch of the imagination be reckoned a "government of the people, by the people, for the people" reformer. He would certainly have the people governed for the people but by those who know not only their business as governors, but who know and are determined to minister to the welfare of the whole state with no other class distinction than that of character. The aim of his experts in social administration would be the organisa-

tion of the forces of social life in such a way as to make it progressively more difficult for the present dead level of stupidity and mediocrity to recur. For it is this low plane of social aspiration and desire that proves the most productive hunting-ground for personally minded demagogues, and Bernard Shaw's attitude towards politics is that of one who will not rest until he has made the people conscious of this. "It annoys me," he says, "to see people comfortable when they ought to be uncomfortable ; and I insist on making them think in order to bring them to conviction of sin." The greatest of all sins is poverty, and it is against this evil that he would have us make war. "The crying need of the nation," he writes, "is not for better morals, cheaper bread, temperance, liberty, culture, redemption of fallen sisters and erring brothers, nor the grace, love, and fellowship of the Trinity ; but simply for enough money. And the evil to be attacked is not sin, suffering, greed, priestcraft, kingcraft, demagogy, monopoly, ignorance, drink, war, pestilence, nor

any other of the scapegoats which reformers sacrifice, but simply poverty." Although he looks at present to the middle classes for the provision of capable leaders in this crusade, his aim is no mere class aim, at least not in so far as the classes are constituted to-day. The middle class has administrative experience and power, in its modern money-form ; these he would conduct into that service whose first aim is the abolition of poverty. His socialism is the conscious nationalisation of human service in the cause of a fuller and deeper life ; a life based on power and ability rather than on weakness and humility ; the creation of a state in which the freedom of the individual shall be coincident with the desire for the greatest social consciousness and the largest human power. The satisfaction of the fundamental material needs of the democracy is the first step in this great aim ; then Shaw looks to a consciously directed evolution eliminating from society that element, which he, following Swift, stigmatises as " the Yahoo," whose vote would otherwise wreck the Commonwealth.

Photograph   Frederick H. Evans.

yours

G. Bernard Shaw

1894

III

THE PLAYWRIGHT

The claim of art to our respect must stand or fall with the validity of its pretension to cultivate and refine our senses and faculties until seeing, hearing, feeling, smelling, and tasting become highly conscious and critical acts with us, protesting vehemently against ugliness, noise, discordant speech, frowsy clothing, and foul air, and taking keen interest and pleasure in beauty, in music, and in the open air, besides making us insist, as necessary for comfort and decency, on clean, wholesome, handsome fabrics to wear, and utensils of fine material and elegant workmanship to handle. Further, art should refine our sense of character and conduct, of justice and sympathy, greatly heightening our self-knowledge, self-control, precision of action, and considerateness, and making us intolerant of baseness, cruelty, injustice, and intellectual superficiality or vulgarity. The worthy artist or craftsman is he who responds to this cultivation of the physical or moral senses by feeding them with pictures, musical compositions, pleasant houses and gardens, good clothes and fine implements, poems, fictions, essays, and dramas, which call the heightened senses and ennobled faculties into pleasurable activity. The greatest artist is he who goes a step beyond the demand, and, by supplying works of a higher beauty and a higher interest than have yet been perceived, succeeds, after a brief struggle with its strangeness, in adding this fresh extension of sense to the heritage of the race. This is why we value art : this is why we feel that the iconoclast and the Puritan are attacking something made holier, by solid usefulness, than their own theories of purity ; this is why art has won the privileges of religion ; so that London shopkeepers who would fiercely resent a compulsory church rate, who do not know "Yankee Doodle" from "God save the Queen," and who are more interested in the photograph of the latest celebrity than in the Velasquez portraits in the National Gallery, tamely allow the London County Council to spend their money on bands, on municipal art inspectors, and on plaster casts from the antique. (In *Liberty*, New York, 27th July, 1895.)

III

THE PLAYWRIGHT

THE deduction to be made from what has been written in the foregoing pages is that Bernard Shaw is an artist with a difference. He is as free of the conventional artistic scruples as he is of the popular artistic follies. He is an artist without being artistic, and one is forced into the belief that he would drop art without the least compunction if it did not aid him in his preaching. Shaw is a preacher of philosophy first, an artist afterwards. But although he has no scruples about the use he would make of art, he does not confuse this personal matter with its real nature. Because he uses art to disseminate a philosophy, he does not commit the error of the moralist who announces that the end of

art is to teach. Neither does he yield comfort to the æsthetically afflicted people who are under the equally prevalent illusion that art is the pursuit of beauty. Beauty is no more likely to occur in art because it is sought than happiness would occur in life for a like reason. Both beauty and happiness are the incidentals of true action. They are the very will-o'-the-wisps of any definite search.

Art, for Shaw, is something closely related to good workmanship. It is the craftsmanship of emotional and imaginative conceptions, having, in so far as its expression is worthy and thorough, a tendency to impel those that come in contact with it towards a similar thoroughness and worthiness of the faculties it affects. It is this power of profoundly moving people which revealed to Shaw the immense propaganda value of art. And he has deliberately used art for philosophical and political ends, just as the Church, perhaps less consciously, used art for religious ends. What art there is in his work stands in the same perspective to the vital thought of to-day as

The Playwright

the Madonnas and holy men in the canvases of the old masters stood in relation to what was vital in the thought of their day. Or to take a more obvious parallel, the Problem Plays of Bernard Shaw, and for the matter of that of Ibsen, Tolstoy, and all who have made problem the life of their drama, are the modern substitutes for the Morality and Mystery Plays of the past. A simple age, with a clear and definite outlook upon life, based upon a re-signed acquiescence in human limitations of perception and power, naturally produced a drama which took the complexion of its formal mind. Hence those dramas whose action was a conflict between personified vices and virtues, and plays that were an exposition of a simple faith in an infinity whose nature should be revealed as a reward for diligence in the pursuit of virtue.

Modernity is, externally at all events, a more complex thing. Formal morals, no less than formal mystery, have given place to philosophic doubt on the one hand and philosophic specula-tion on the other. We breathe a problematic

atmosphere. We are no longer content to whisper "mystery" with awe-stricken reverence. The mystery of life is becoming irksome, just as morality has become a prison. We want to know more and to experience more. The air is quick with demands for new standards and for fresh valuations of the old conceptions of right and wrong. And although the infinite has not capitulated to human need, morality is on the eve of being accounted finite. So the vital dramatic need of the day forces this state of problem upon the stage. In Ibsen it raises the curtain upon society during typical moments of actuality, showing us the struggles of the will to be free. The drama of Tolstoy is an endeavour to breathe into the same circumstance a new and passionate realisation of the flagging spirit of Christianity. And in Bernard Shaw's plays we have personal volition made the hero of a drama that is conscious of the critical values of its own action. His characters live in an atmosphere which is constantly, though not always directly, expository. Shaw's drama is the only consistently

The Playwright

religious drama of the day—it is as relentless in its pursuit of an exalted idea as were the ancient Moralities and Mysteries. But his morality does not appeal from the standard to the man, but from the man to the standard. His moral hero does not say, as Goodness and Virtue said in the old plays, "Behold, I am good because I am like goodness," but "Behold, I am good because I am myself." And in the same way his mystic hero is no longer before a God whom man as man could never see, but he is none the less in the face of mystery. The modern mystic, the hero of Shaw's drama, does not stand before a veil which hides him from his God, he stands in the midst of a set of circumstances which are vital with the energy of a God who is no longer God but the Life Force, and his whole aim is to make this force his own. He is no longer a child asking for guidance, but an adult demanding his rights, and acting on his own responsibility. His inquisitiveness will no longer be satisfied with a symbol—it wants the thing itself.

Bernard Shaw

The attitude of such a hero, who, like all heroes, is born out of his due time, must be critical. It is really the critical side of Bernard Shaw that has imposed itself most obviously upon his characters. Shaw's most obvious attitude towards society is, of course, critical, and all his plays are criticisms. They are the flower and consummation of the famous *Saturday Review* articles which were ostensibly dramatic criticisms, but actually criticisms of life—a function continued in the plays. His most constant demand was for the restoration of life to the stage, and he did not spare the purveyors of those substitutes for reality, which then and now almost monopolise the theatre. To Bernard Shaw the theatre is the temple, if not of the Holy Ghost, at least of the Holy Spirit—the soul of all that is responsible and vital in life. It is a place where intellect and imagination should interpret life to men, show them the reality they could not see otherwise, and what is more, help them to realise their own relationship to that reality. His whole dramatic

The Playwright

criticism is a demand (and his plays are a contribution to its fulfilment) for a drama that will show us the effect of genuine human action, and not of action frustrated and veiled at every point by traditional conceptions of conduct or artificial acceptances of things as they are supposed to be and not as they are.

It is critical because it is alive. It is the creation not merely of a will to live, but of a will to live masterfully. It is informed, incisive, passionate, and quite direct for those who are mentally alert enough to grasp a fresh view of ideas. It is even amusing for those who have not this faculty. But here we come in contact with Shavian humour, which has been his undoing for many good people. The mind that has been fed on the philosophy of the schoolmen, that has been engaged with the tedious dullness of ideas in the abstract, can only with great difficulty understand that philosophy applied to life and expressed by art is not only a very real thing, but also an enjoyable thing. Bernard Shaw has the gift of

expression by art : but he has not the gift of concealing himself in his art, although he manages to conceal his seriousness from the superficial observer. This does not mean that he is not elusive. From one point of view he is as baffling as the pea under the conjurer's thimbles, and with equally logical reasons. But his position is clear in the mass if not in every detail. It is just these logical points that may be at the root of all the trouble. Shaw's mind is as relentless as Euclid. His inner vision, however, is quick to see the humour of this process, and as the logical mind ploughs through conventions and traditions, it is quick to seize and assert itself. So are born the anti-climax and paradox which set the world laughing and the wise thinking as well.

His art has been an evolution towards a means of expression, for the sake of propaganda, a means which he could use with increasing freedom and effectiveness. Students of his works can detect this development, through the essay and the novel, to that propaganda by drama which has at length

impressed, if not convinced, his contemporaries. In fact, in his "nonage," when he produced the series of more or less still-born novels, these products bore many of the characteristics of the stage-play. They were largely carried on by means of dialogue interspersed with the minimum of description and the maximum of explanation—in which last he has always been a master. These novels were really embryonic stage-plays, transitional drama ; and what actually happened, when they became the genuine article, was a rearrangement of their parts rather than an alteration in their matter. The descriptions became the scenario, amplified before each act in the printed plays ; the explanation became the now famous prefaces and appendices, or else formed a considerable and increasing part of the dialogue which, with little alteration, conveyed the action in much the same way as it did in the novel—a form of art which, by the way, has been called the pocket theatre.

Perhaps his main reason for adopting the

art of drama, in spite of what he has said to the contrary, was the obvious one of suitability to temperament. For every good speaker has something histrionic in his composition, and the drama is the natural art medium for its expression. But with this desire for a medium of expression that would readily impress masses of people with the ideas he had at heart, there was the dramatic reformer's wish to introduce to the British stage an element which might help in restoring a desirable high seriousness to an art which is gradually replacing the Church in our religious life. As a dramatist his aim was to produce plays that were free from the romantic conceptions which have gathered round all the important functions of life : to express life realistically, that is, from his own point of view. He has laboured to create a drama, not for the voluptuary, nor for the idle amusement of ordinary people, nor for the delectation of those who wish to see recorded obvious incidents and outworn beliefs, but a drama that would stimulate the intelligence to a lively

concern with all the near and far details of social life.

The stage in England, save for the bright interlude of the Gilbert and Sullivan comic-opera, was bathed in that sentimental glamour which had suffused the nineteenth century from its dawn. But the gush of tears that heralded its birth was like to be replaced by a cynicism as futile if not quite so absurd. It was the drama of useless action produced with the direct purpose of exploiting those to whom useful action was impossible. All the ingenuity of clever playwrights and cleverer actors was wasted upon an interminable series of shallow heroics concerning man's desire for woman, relieved by those equally clever and equally futile farcical comedies whose capacity for "still running" seemed to be their most laudable feature.

It was in the midst of the self-complacency of this state of things that the bombshell of Ibsen burst, whose reverberations are heard down to to-day. These were renewed quite recently in New York, when pretty much the

same hysterical epithets of outraged respectability were hurled at Shaw on the production of *Mrs. Warren's Profession*, as were hurled at Ibsen when *Ghosts* was first played in England by the Stage Society. The critics were bewildered, and their outraged sense of decorum expressed itself in such a tirade of indignant vituperation as never before filled a newspaper column. Criticism was thrown overboard, and in its stead we had a wild crescendo of hysterical abuse, culminating in the horrified cry of the late Mr. Clement Scott, who, exhausting the vocabulary of journalistic wrath, threw down his burning pen after declaring the play to be "an open drain." The American critics were hardly less abusive in their criticisms of *Mrs. Warren's Profession* than were the English critics of *Ghosts*. To one it was "a most designedly useless and prurient comedy"; to another it was "illuminated gangrene," whilst a third cried out for disinfectants.

It must be recognised, however, that in spite of its absurdity, such criticism has a basis in a

very genuine feeling, which is rather flamboy-
antly voiced by the critical mentors of the Press.
It is the feeling of a very large class in a country
like England, where, as well as the millions who
have to put up with conditions of poverty, there
are millions, ranging from the moderately comfortable to the moderately rich, whose habit
of perpetual money-making has atrophied or
destroyed the habit of philosophic thought,
and whose more or less certain condition of
mechanical comfort and luxury strongly re-
sents any criticism either derogatory of or
dangerous to its settled habits. This is the
novel-reading, newspaper-reading, theatre-
going public, and most commercially successful
literature and art is the expression of its
ideals and prejudices.

This is really the dominant class in English
life ; it is more class-conscious, more assertive
both morally and religiously, more energetic
and vigorous in pursuit of its ambitions, than
is either the class below or the class above.
It is, therefore, all the more difficult to move
it from any path which it has grown to con-

sider worthy. Its beliefs and aspirations are reflected in the popular art of the day; in the literature at the front of the bookstalls and "in demand" at the libraries; in the plays with long-date bookings for the stalls and long-petticoated *queues* for the pit; in the pictures at Burlington House that are honoured with double-page reproductions in the weekly illustrated papers; in the music of the "popular" ballad concert and the "light" opera. And in all this art a certain standard, what its devotees would probably call "tone," is noticeable. The more humble of these will speak of it as "toney," and the more authoritative and successful, but none the less incapable of a sound opinion, as "awfully jolly," and "quite alright." And all the critics in the pay of this middle class will form a chorus, chiming in with columns of approved and modulated cadenzas in the key of "quite alright."

This particular tone that is so popular is unerring in its certainty. It has a little eternity of its own, with a compact little faith and a whole hierarchy of priests and acolytes

attendant upon its thought-proof deities. To
these deities, of course, its appeal is perpetual
and faithful—and the deities, after the manner
of their kind, return the compliment with
mute indifference ; till in the end, the
devotees, after the manner of devotees, use
their deities as cloaks to hide their own insufficiency. The sanctity of the family and of
the home, for instance, has become a protecting
cloud about the sentimental tyrannies of hus-
bands, wives, and children, each striving to
obtain and control the other, and resulting in
a nebulous and shallow indifference to everything but externals and names. Education,
another favoured god, becomes the systematic
curriculum-cramming of the young—the intellectual slaughter of the innocents—with
what result ? A rising generation and a generation just risen with no further intelligence
than an infinite capacity for being deceived.
And to name but one more—Democracy—
the people's will : expressing itself for ever in
the faded and tawdry pomp and circumstance
of an outworn feudalism ; lauding its free and

popular institutions to the skies, and using what privileges it possesses, grudgingly or not at all, at the dictation of the stale rhetoric of politicians.

The relationship of Bernard Shaw's plays to this state of affairs is that of diagnosis. They are a critical and dramatic statement of social disease, and his diagnosis has been gradually freeing itself from the somewhat crude expression of the views of a social physician in the early plays, whose emphatic sociology was almost too much for the dramatic idea. But in his latest phase, bare sociology is relegated to the preface or appendix, where it takes the form of commentation upon the philosophic contest which now holds his stage. At the same time, his plays have always been of the one category. They have always enunciated one set purpose, and what change can be denoted is one of point of view rather than of idea ; it is the rapid evolution of a mind from an economic to a philosophic interpretation of life. It exhibits an intelligence that has not ceased to look entirely with

the eye, but now looks through the eye as well. And side by side with a growing sense of the mystic element in life his powerful visual sense of things as they are has increased rather than otherwise.

The sociological are practically the *unpleasant* plays, though *The Philanderer* is more in the nature of an anticipation of the later method of expository comedy. *Mrs. Warren's Profession* and *Widowers' Houses* are pure social science dramatised. So little of the later philosophic wit do they contain, that they represent Shaw's nearest approach to dullness. Their method is that of pictorial dialogue exhibiting certain evils in the social strata by making an intellectual appeal to the emotions. But in the intermediate period, which is anticipated in the character of Frank in *Mrs. Warren's Profession*, the method is that of illumination by examples in action. It is in these plays that his creative faculty has given most delight; in the *pleasant* plays Shaw is no longer a scientist, his philosophy is less

aggressive than elsewhere. *You Never Can Tell* and *Candida* are his nearest approaches to impersonality : his criticism of life in these plays is not so obvious. It is there to be sure ; it is obvious to the philosopher in the pit ; but the only impression made on the average mind is one of amused bewilderment, pleasant in its way, with just that note of aggravation caused by the subtlety of a truth of whose existence one is half in doubt.

In these comedies Shaw has achieved creation ; he has made out of words beings that have a distinct existence, beings that are both the embodiment and the interpretation of an idea. He has furthermore created a type— something that is representative. The leading characters in his plays have that distinction which one only associates with the work of the masters of literature. They are Shavian, as Mr. Micawber and Mrs. Gamp are Dickensian, as Sir Willoughby Patterne and Adrian Harley are Meredithian. They bear the temperamental complexion of their creator, yet

The Playwright

live independently in a set of circumstances which are the inevitable outcome of their every action.

There is a Shaw Woman and a Shaw Man, or, rather, a Shaw Boy, and these beings have the habit of all effective art of refusing to be talked out of existence. They withstand argument as nonchalantly as they survive conventional morals. A decade of puzzled criticism leaves Candida and Marchbanks as fresh as when they first met the rebukes and laughter of the public. And so it is with the rest of them, with Cleopatra no less than with Louis Dubedat, with Anne Whitefield, with Dick Dudgeon, with Frank Gardner, and with Valentine, and Mrs. Clandon's incorrigible twins, who have all amused and bewildered, who have all been acclaimed "brilliant" plus the provisional "but." It seems to be the fate of Bernard Shaw to make men laugh, and even in many cases to make them think, but rarely to win other than provisional appreciation. Praise of him is generally qualified with this protective clause, as though

both critic and public were afraid of his "brilliance" and "cleverness" committing them to an acceptance of unorthodox views.

Shaw has stated again and again that his object is, in the fullest sense of a misused word, educational. He has a clear vision of social rectitude, and society's declensions fill him with a puritanical wrath which expresses itself in critical satire and expository declamation woven into the texture of his drama. He has added nothing to stage-craft, nor to the art of play-writing, save a definite and original point of view and the faculty of instilling a new zeal into actors. In structure, the plays differ very little from the ordinary play. His long experience as a dramatic critic has given him a knowledge of all the tricks of the trade, and these he uses with the greatest freedom. What he has severely avoided is the sentimental glamour into which the popular dramatist plunges every action, and what he has aimed at doing for the English stage is what Ibsen, Tolstoy, Strindberg, Brieux, and others have done for the European stage, that is, to

inaugurate a problem drama of modern ideas ; to exhibit dramatically the vital part of human beings struggling against things and conditions, and conceived without any superstitious deference to tradition. For, as he says, " Drama is no mere setting up of the camera to nature : it is the presentation in parable of the conflict between Man's will and his environment : in a word, of problem."

But the most aggressive difference between the Shaw play and that of other playwrights is what appears to be his inhuman indifference to all those sentiments about sex and dignity which society has grown to look upon as sacred. And Shaw's inhumanity to man, in the romantic sense, needs no apology—it is too obvious to be explained away, and too obviously deliberate to be treated other than as intended. This is a point that has raised the ire of the tender-hearted, and set the critics by the ears. The production of plays from a new recipe is, indeed, cause enough to puzzle those who had thought nothing so final as the Shakespearian not-for-a-day-but-for-all-time tradition. But this cold-

ness and apparent lack of human kindness is relative. Bernard Shaw is, indeed, frigid in reference to many of the things that arouse emotional warmth in most people, but this does not mean that he lacks feeling. As a matter of fact, he feels deeply and passionately, but not for the things for which one is usually supposed to feel deeply and passionately. His plays laugh at voluptuousness, when they are not denouncing it, whereas the average play cloaks it in a veil of modesty, always gratifying to the playgoer who diligently permits himself to feel secretly what he would not dream of condoning in public. Hence, when a dramatist comes and pulls away the flimsy veil and shows life from the other side, he naturally seems callous. "The reintroduction of problem," says Shaw, "with its remorseless logic and iron framework of fact inevitably produces at first an overwhelming impression of coldness and inhuman rationalism. But this will soon pass away. When the intellectual muscle and moral nerve of the critics has been developed in the struggle with

modern problem plays, the pettish luxurious-
ness of the clever ones, and the sulky sense
of disadvantaged weakness in the sentimental
ones, will clear away ; and it will be seen that
only in the problem play is there any real
drama." To the modern mind this must be
inevitable if we are to have a vital national
drama. Already there is a class which grows
weary of the eternal recurrence of hackneyed
sex themes, around whose pivot dance the
dozen or so plots which constitute the dramatic
stock-in-trade of our stage. A class is showing signs of existence which demands a drama
that shall not enervate but quicken intelligence;
and the steadily growing audience at the
Vedrenne-Barker performances has proved that
this public is ready to support what it demands.

The nature of the conflict which drama
represents should vary, of course, with every
age. For the conflict, as presented on the
stage, must ultimately resolve itself into a
struggle between man and the manners and
conditions of the period in which he exists.
Finally it becomes the struggle of man against

the obstacles between him and his desires—between man and what he wants. These wants, when reduced to their essence, are nothing short of life itself. Whether it be food or money or love, it is all the same. Our wants are but points at which we become conscious of life. They complete, as it were, the circle of the conscious and sub-conscious, giving the flash which is the taste of eternity. No conflict between man and his environment can occur without the interposition of man's will. It is the clash of will and environment that constitutes drama, whether the environment be some impalpable destiny as in the Greek Drama, some overwhelming conception of moral obligation as in the Shakespearian, or the narrowing ideals and institutions of an outworn society as in Ibsen and Tolstoy.

The place of Bernard Shaw's plays is in the last category. Yet they are distinct both from those of Tolstoy and Ibsen, who achieve, it must be confessed, an impersonality never attained by Shaw. Ibsen never philosophises, Shaw rarely does anything else. In his most

impersonal situations the cloven hoof of the propagandist is evident. You look at *A Doll's House* in that nonplussed way in which you contemplate life. *Candida* creates quite a different impression; in this play you are uncertain as to whether you are in the presence of life or not; yet in spite of the fact that you are not convinced you feel vexed, for you are tempted to believe that you fail to do so through lack of intelligence. Now this tempter is a fact—it is Shaw tugging your intellect towards his point of view. It is as though the possible symbolism of the door through which Nora Helmer in *A Doll's House* goes to her freedom were to become a subtle undertone of moral comment throughout the play. It is symbolism explaining itself. Ibsen shows you men and women in conflict with personalities, conduct, and tradition, free of all comment; he rings up the curtain and shows you social life at psychological moments. Shaw does something else. He sees life quite as sharply as Ibsen does, he states what he sees with the same acute sense of fact, but he can-

not or will not entirely separate it from his own explanatory mind. He rings up the curtain and *explains* social life. Where Ibsen is a simple realist Shaw is an expository realist— he is Ibsen become self-conscious.

But it is not finally in comparison with Ibsen that the true Shaw may be discovered. Rather may one hope to do so in comparison with Shakespear—with that Shakespear in connection with whom there has been so much misunderstanding of Shaw. For after all, different as are Shaw and Ibsen, there is that kinship between them born of a common *zeitgeist* which does not belong to the Elizabethan and the modern dramatists. We must, in the first place, abandon the popular belief that Bernard Shaw is attitudinising when he criticises Shakespear. He is endeavouring as lucidly as a clever pen and an almost supernatural wit will allow him to be sincerely and sanely critical. In the second place, we must abandon the idea that Shaw seeks on every occasion to disparage Shakespear. This is simply not true, and there are many passages

The Playwright

in his *Saturday Review* criticisms in which he appreciates Shakespear quite as eloquently as those who consider it sacrilege to criticise the bard ; as, for instance, when he speaks of *Twelfth Night* and *A Midsummer Night's Dream* as "crown jewels of dramatic poetry," and of *All's Well that Ends Well* being rooted in his "deeper affections." Even in the famous *Better than Shakespear?* preface to *Three Plays for Puritans*, he says that no man "will ever write a better tragedy than Lear," and again, in a letter to the *Daily News*, 17th April, 1905, he says : " In manner and art nobody can write better than Shakespear, because, carelessness apart, he did the thing as well as it can be done within the limits of human faculty," which all goes to prove at least that Shaw is not an indiscriminating critic ; and further, his genuine interest in Shakespear is always exemplified in the severe handling he gives those popularisers of the plays who cut and prettify them out of all recognition to suit public taste. His antagonism is not so much towards the bard as towards what he terms

Bardolatry. Judicious readers of his prefaces will recognise that his act is not an act of false criticism, but of justifiable iconoclasm.

The point to recognise at the outset is that a high quality of execution is not peculiar to genius. Perfect execution is possible to any tyro with sufficient staying power to master the constructive details of a craft. Sometimes, indeed, fineness of execution is not even the result of a talent for perseverance— it is a trick. In every age there are practitioners as clever as the masters. What finally counts is the depth of passion which informs the work of one who knows his business, be he artist or merchant. It is this that constitutes the master. It is the working of what Shaw calls "That fruitful, contained, governed, instinctively utilised passion which makes nations and individuals great," and not the superficial dexterity of the dilettante.

With Shakespear's dazzling ability Shaw has no further quarrel than that this power of rhetoric has been the cause of the hero-worship which has paralysed frank criticism. For

in spite of the fact that playwrights and managers have never ceased modifying, adapting, and taking other liberties with the canonical works, the transcendent eloquence and narrative powers of these same works have so dominated even the best minds, that not only these qualities but the very morality and attitude towards life of the age which they so superlatively represent, have become canonised and invested with inviolability. It is the fact that Shakespear is no longer a sane belief, but a superstition, which has sent Shaw into the public place with words of wrath and warning.

Half of Shaw's so-called attack upon Shakespear is the old antagonism of the free mind with the academic mind. It is the never-ending struggle of faith, will, volition with their ancient enemy, tradition. It is the immemorial war between the bond and the free, between the mind that accepts and the mind that creates. In Shaw it is that tenet of his faith which says that "The Golden Rule is that there are no golden rules," expressing

itself in terms of art criticism. For, he says, "the severity of artistic discipline is produced by the fact that in creative art no ready-made rules can help you, there is nothing to guide you to the right expression for your thought except your own sense of beauty and fitness; and, as you advance upon those who went before you, that sense of beauty and fitness is necessarily often in conflict, not with fixed rules, because there are no rules, but with precedents."

Progress has only been possible by the constant challenging of current conditions, intellectual, spiritual, or temporal. The challenge of what is accepted and fixed is the only protection life knows against decay, for there is no permanence. What is not constantly moving towards the more desirable must be receding towards what is less desirable. Finality in politics, religion, or art is illusion. "Where there are no graves, there are no resurrections." Progress is always accompanied by the fall of an institution, the repudiation of a church, or the negation of an academy. It is the institu-

tion of a final authority that creates revolution. This is nature's reply to a transgression of her laws. Bernard Shaw's attitude towards Shakespear has been necessitated by the existence of a Shakespearean institution; for institutions only spring up where there is, as Thoreau says, "a lull of truth." Shaw sees that so long as Shakespear is recognised as the final authority in drama there can be no more possibility of growth in that art than there could be in the mind of man under the jurisdiction of an authoritative theocracy.

But this is only one side of his heresy. The other is the undoing of the meshes into which the Shakespearean tradition has cast the native drama. The criticism he makes of Shakespear might easily have been made by Shakespear upon those ideas which persisted in hampering the free expression of what was modern under the Renaissance. For all live art is the outcome of the age in which it is born. Idolatry of Shakespear not only prevents a true appreciation of his defects, but it increases the chances of their being mistaken

for his good qualities. Worse still, it gives rise to that imitative dabbling which in the end obscures the true greatness of the original. As Shaw has pointed out, " It was the age of gross ignorance of Shakespear and incapacity for his works that produced the indiscriminate eulogies with which we are familiar. It was the revival of genuine criticism of those works that coincided with the movement for giving genuine instead of spurious and silly representations of his plays."

Masterpieces are only "final for their epoch," because they can only be the expressions of a philosophy of life peculiar to their epoch. That is why Shaw demands a drama free of Shakespearean idolatry; and not only a drama, but art in all its branches, illuminating the age with the light of its own ripe ideas. For it is obvious that what was true for the Elizabethans is no longer so for us. The whole world is changed. The epoch begun then has reached its culminating point, and is no longer in the ascendant. Their faiths are our superstitions, and they would long ago

have found a decent repose had not their
ghosts been unnaturally cajoled to walk the
night across that last refuge of defunct ideas,
the British stage. The serious point is, the
fact that since our average man must take his
opinions from somewhere, having not yet
acquired the art of forming his own, and being
no longer willing to accept those distributed
from the pulpit, he has no recourse but to the
press and the stage. As the former is largely
controlled by the same gentlemen who are interested in the conservation of the sixteenth-
century romanticism of the latter, it has come
about that the long-suffering public is led to
believe that the age of chivalry is still with us,
though its actions affirm the contrary a thou-
sand times a day.

Bernard Shaw's adverse criticism of Shakespear is the most obvious side of his antagonism to romanticism generally; to the point
of view that is consistent in its vision but
inconsistent in its deduction; to the mind
which can grasp a reality, but will not accept
it unless it is dressed romantically; and par-

ticularly to that extensive field of romantic energy which finds expression in the affection of the sexes. And since his most incisive words on the subject have been part and parcel of his dramatic criticism, it was to be expected of him that when he became a dramatist himself his plays would, at any rate, tend towards the establishment of an unromantic drama in this country. And this is just what his plays are. They stand to drama in much the same way as Whitman's *Leaves of Grass* stand to poetry. They are not the usual conventional thing, not the polished article beloved of the virtuosi and demanded by the schools. Shaw and Whitman possess both drama and poetry equal in the recognised way to the best work of the accepted masters. But Shaw's plays and Whitman's poems are alike tentative; they are hints and even something more than hints; they are suggestions and indications of the work of poet and playwright to come.

As the sentimental romance which dominates the stage has been the chief negation of Shaw's criticism of the stage, it was natural that out

The Playwright

of this should spring his plays. These have demonstrated that interesting stage plays can be made in which the love interest is a phase among other important and interesting phases of the drama of life. And in one play particularly, and in others incidentally, he has shown that there can be dramatic force, interest, and truth in a situation in which the unromantic conception of masculine subjection to feminine passion and privilege is made a central theme.

Although this stand against the romance of love is taken up in each of his plays, it finds a special voice in *Cæsar and Cleopatra* which is a deliberate challenge to the Shakespearean tradition. And not only a challenge, he candidly offers his Cæsar as an improvement on Shakespear's, at the same time claiming for himself the right Shakespear claimed when he interpreted Cæsar and Brutus according to his own light and not that of Plutarch; or later, as Mommsen and Carlyle have each realised the same and other historical facts in the light of their own philosophy of life,

regardless of conflict with previous conceptions. It must be noted that Shaw does not offer his Cæsar and his Cleopatra as the conceptions of his age : they are presented simply as his own conceptions. He deals with past history in just the same spirit as with present, with neither more nor less reverence. His Cæsar is clever, masterful, unscrupulous, a philosopher and a man of action, and not a pompous and heroic simulacrum. His Cleopatra, a girl in years, a child in wilfulness, is a woman in cunning. Love is an incident in the life of Cæsar, a means to an end in that of Cleopatra. And each figure in the play talks and acts with the spontaneous inevitability of human beings of any epoch. But in addition to this and as a substitute for the prescribed activity of the traditional stage heroes, the theatrical picture-photographs which have been handed down to us by each succeeding age of dramatists, we have a new precedent. Bernard Shaw himself steps upon the stage. He enters into the minds of all his characters, and adds his own definitely modern note to the careful realism

of the theme. It is ancient history born anew after the trials and tribulations, the experiences and thoughts of hundreds of intervening years. Cæsar talks like Shaw, and becomes more like Cæsar. Cleopatra prattles like a pampered and peevish girl, and reveals the eternal feminine. Ptolemy is a boy with the years of his forbears weighing him down. It is in reality not the representation of history. It is not merely, as Shaw would have us accept it, the treatment of men and women as natural history. It is a new light thrown upon history. It is history revived by the aid of the intensity of recollected experiences,—the experiences that have come between the ages, that are always in process of reforming the mind and feelings of succeeding years. Bernard Shaw has focussed the light of the ages as construed in himself, and revealed us a new world in the old and an old world in the new.

With the repudiation of romantic love must be coupled Shaw's other great heresy— the renunciation of the idea of duty. It is these two negations which form the staple

critical ingredients of the plays. Their existence lies behind his creative faculty. They
are the parents of all those children of his
imagination, those distinctly Shavian types,
whose existence in his plays are among the
most distinct facts of recent art. Shaw has
embodied his ideas of unromantic dutiless
man in human forms, and his drama is the
conflict of these individuals with the non-
Shavian type—that is, with the average type
of man. This is the fundamental action of
his plays.

The great danger of such a method is the
possible over-emphasis of the characteristics
of their author so as to draw the interest of
the spectators from the drama to him. This,
it must be admitted, has happened in Shaw's
case, and there is imminent danger of his
ideas being altogether lost in the enthusiasm
for the Shavian expression of the thing rather
than for the thing itself. And though all his
characters are oratorically Shaws, he has gone
out of his way on at least two occasions, in
the stage representations of *Man and Superman*,

The Playwright

and in *The Admirable Bashville*, to allow a photographic resemblance of himself to help the easy illusion.

Yet when Shaw is not embodying his philosophy of life in a character but merely using his wonderful gift of observation, he can delineate men and women with all the definiteness of great art. One of his characters at least—the famous old waiter in *You Never Can Tell*—may be claimed to rank with the supreme humorous conceptions of literature. But such work is not Shaw's aim. The dominance of his intellect and his tendency towards wit rather than humour would make it difficult for him to create those enduring humorous types which help to make the art of fiction tolerable — Falstaff and Corporal Trim, Gargantua, Tartarin, Pickwick, Richmond-Roy. These are, in fact, the masterpieces of that romantic era which the plays of Bernard Shaw renounce—but never denounce. Shaw is the critic of his period, and not its caricaturist. His renunciation is too complete for that. To be a good

caricaturist one must be in love with the thing burlesqued. One must not seek to abolish the thing itself, but only its follies. This is the real difference between the satirist and the caricaturist, between the revolutionary critic and the conservative critic, between Bernard Shaw and, say, W. S. Gilbert, a dramatist who has shown as much originality from one point of view as Shaw has from another. For Gilbert must be recognised as a distinctive feature in our modern drama, as one of the very rare features, along with the J. M. Barrie of *The Admirable Crichton*, the W. B. Yeats of *Where There is Nothing*, and with Oscar Wilde; not to do more than mention the younger generation of modern playwrights as exemplified in the splendid work of men like Granville Barker, John Galsworthy, and John Masefield, which is, properly speaking, the first fruit of the new era.

If we take then, for instance, the Gilbertian and the Shavian treatment of the conception of duty, we shall arrive at something like the truth of the matter. Duty to the conserva-

tive Gilbert is a desirable thing, in moderation; it is the fanaticism of duty which he abhors. To exhibit the folly of this he creates a series of ingenious incidents in which duty is pushed to an absurdity—as in the diverting burlesque, *The Pirates of Penzance*. Now the revolutionary Shaw, who has no illusions about the value of duty, seeks to abolish it altogether. He therefore does not attempt to make duty look ridiculous by exaggeration; this from his point of view is supererogatory. He simply creates a figure who is free of all subservience to the convention and sets him in action among the dutiful—as in the incidents throughout his plays, but in a more concrete form in *Major Barbara*.

The main difference between the Shavian and the Gilbertian play is that, in the former, life in its ordinary channels is looked upon in much the same way as in the latter in its extraordinary channels. Shaw fears the dangers of the normal—Gilbert of the abnormal. This is why Gilbert always writes burlesque-comedy and Shaw tragi-comedy. One laughs happily

with the author of *Patience*, but with the author of *Major Barbara* one laughs sadly. The laughter of the one is produced by a desirable excess of the comforts of civilisation. It is the dwellers in a right little, tight little island making merry over the tolerable defects of an on-the-whole lovable little system. It is the self-satisfied side glance of highly civilised people. It is, in fact, Meredith's "oblique ray" in action ; the result is comedy, and it awakens, as the great novelist expected of comedy, "thoughtful laughter," with the thought part of it, judging by results, not very deep.

Now Shaw also throws the oblique ray upon institutions, but he is not like Gilbert, on the whole, a supporter of these institutions. On the whole, he is their arch-enemy. His comedy provokes the laughter of the mind also. It is designed for this purpose, but not for this purpose alone. It does not aim at laughter as an end in itself. It does not aim at producing a state of hilarity which is happily intolerant and contentedly impotent. It

The Playwright

would make you laugh by stinging you into something better ; it would make thoughtful laughter the prelude to thoughtful act. That action does not always follow is the tragic side of his comedy and the tragedy of his propaganda.

The plays of Bernard Shaw are tragi-comedies conceived in the form of dialogue with dramatic interludes. Most of them would answer to his description of *Major Barbara*, which he frankly called a " discussion." The tendency latterly has been towards this element. Discussion has become the predominant partner in the dramatic arrangement —indeed, the action has become discussion. As Shaw has grown towards mysticism his plays have become more static. His characters talk dynamics, but they do next to nothing. The point to realise here is that his discussions still retain that interest without which the drama would fail in its object—they are still dramatic. But the action is no longer the conflict between men and things, nor yet between man and man. It is a conflict of

ideas as expressed in varying temperaments and by differing wills. His characters do not kill each other, neither do they kill themselves; material force has become akin to annotation rather than theme. They talk to each other—they discuss.

Shaw has introduced philosophic dialogue into the activity of the stage, and the audience has stayed to listen. And it would not be an extravagant thing to say that he would allow material action to drop out altogether without the least reluctance could he keep his auditorium full without it.[1] This does not mean the annihilation of drama. He has done dramatically in another way what Maeterlinck did for the spirit of man. He has created a static drama of the intelligence, which can be quite as dramatic as the most intense incidents in the dramatic idea which gave us *Aglavaine et Selysette* and *Le mort de Tintagiles*.

[1] A fact accomplished in the recent production of the philosophic interlude from *Man and Superman*, under the title, *Don Juan in Hell*, at the Royal Court Theatre. Here the static conditions are maintained throughout; so much so that hardly a critic in London could contain his indignation—nevertheless, the theatre was filled with an attentive and appreciative audience for many matinees.

The Playwright

The dramatic moments in his plays thrill with a difference. It is not the thrill of pent-up emotion. It is the altogether new thrill experienced by those who come in contact with a reality which is familiar but strange. It is unlike the alleged realities of romantic drama, with its purple patches of battle, murder, and sudden death. It is the sudden realisation of all those feelings and thoughts which have never been brought under vivid observation. The great surprises of Shaw's drama are the sincere actions of more or less ordinary people.

This action, which began as sociological drama, has become philosophical drama. His men and women are no longer mere types of a nation of shopkeepers. They are symbols of the world-will. The conflict in his plays is now like the focussed point at which the contact of inflammable objects with the sun-rays through a convex glass produces fire—only for sun-rays we have will-power. The quintessence of Shaw's plays is the concentration of will into the energy of life.

There is no doubt that in his early plays he had only a vague idea of the theme which he has eventually made his own. In *Mrs. Warren's Profession* there was a momentary anticipation of the seemingly perverse views of the later stage. But as his view of life has developed his drama has changed accordingly. What in *Widowers' Houses* and *Mrs. Warren's Profession* is an expression of the reformer's zeal plus an exceedingly acute power of observation; what in *Arms and the Man, You Never Can Tell,* and *Captain Brassbound's Conversion* is a keen sense of satiric comedy plus the moral revolutionist's contempt for conventional manners; becomes in *Man and Superman, Major Barbara,* and *The Doctor's Dilemma* the expression of a view of life which has by no means lost either its reformer's zeal, its revolutionist's scorn, or its power of observation, but has added to these an insight penetrating deep below surfaces and a philosophy embracing the whole of human life.

The early anticipations appeared in the

The Playwright

whimsical activity, the almost elfish wilfulness of such characters as Frank in *Mrs. Warren's Profession*; the Twins and Valentine in *You Never Can Tell*; Marchbanks in *Candida*, coupled with the strange power of such women as Candida, in the same play, and Lady Cecily Waynflete in *Captain Brassbound's Conversion*. The unexpected always happened with these people; they did things that were different from the usual, so different as to be ranked as unnatural. Now, as a matter of fact, these figures are not unnatural at all. They are simply people acting from quite natural as distinct from conventional motives. They are people doing what they like to do and what they can do for their own reasons, which is no reason, and not as in the ordinary romantic way in deference to some preconceived ideal.

These characters were the forerunners of the genuine Shaw conception of Man, who is really undeveloped Superman. His first appearance was in *The Devil's Disciple*, in the part of Dick Dudgeon, who steps on to the

stage surrounded by all the appurtenances of histrionic romance, and does just what he wants to do, following the opposite to the conventional God, the Devil, and succeeding in being the only really lovable character in the play. In life, Shaw would have us observe, the lovable beings are the self-centred, those who act from their own initiative in their own way. Their power is infectious just as weakness is, but to infect with power is to bring joy, even though the world rocks with the effort.

Dick Dudgeon is the real Shaw hero—the man who knows what he wants and wills his way to it. He reappears in another form as Andrew Undershaft in *Major Barbara*, the incarnation of self-expression rather than self-suppression, the sign of the Sword as distinct from the sign of the Cross. It is not necessary, however, that the activity of these embryonic supermen should be towards the social ends desired by Shaw. The final aim is that they should be strong, self-balanced, free, capable of willing and acting—the rest will

The Playwright

follow. Even the misplaced activity of the conquering Anglo-Saxon Broadbent in *John Bull's Other Island* is better than the ineffectual bickerings of the peasantry for ever building ideals which they never realise are prisons.

But the spirit which dominates the figures in Shaw's plays is growing further removed from that which is the impelling motive in other plays, or, rather, it is becoming more and more conscious of its own importance. His hero is no longer a man; it is the Life Force finding expression, as it did in Ibsen, in the "recognition of an eternally womanly principle in the universe." Women appear in his plays in an entirely new light. They no longer submit prettily to man's fabled dominance, but man finally succumbs to theirs. The cosy passivity of domestic romance is replaced by an activity informed with a new and critical cunning: the power of a great element being consciously used for the first time. Lovableness and womanliness are no longer romantic charms to be eagerly sought and cherished by

infatuated males; they charm certainly, but by
the same means that predatory animals attract
their quarry. They are the protective colour-
ing of nature's creative needs, civilised and
moralised, so that he who comes within their
power can no longer call himself his own. He
is henceforth their disillusioned slave and
their owner's property.

Shaw expresses the contrary idea to that interpreted by Meredith in *The Egoist*. Clara
Middleton flies from the overbearing egoism
of Sir Willoughby Patterne, but it is woman
who is the conqueror in *Man and Superman*
and man the defeated. For John Tanner,
after struggling as passionately for his liberty
as romantic lovers struggle for the thraldom
of love, at length capitulates to the Life Force
in the person of Ann Whitefield under protest, in the grip of a power beyond his control.
This power is Nature consolidating her permanence by the instrumentality of sex in its
most patient, cunning, and captivating form—
woman. Ann, whom we are informed is every-
woman though every woman is not Ann, is the

direct ally of the Life Force unscrupulously determined in its set purpose and wildly jealous of all competing purposes, and Tanner is a precocious dawning of the world-will striving to maintain the concentrative force of its energy in his personality for objects other than home and babies.

Man and Superman is a modern version of the fall of man. It is man resisting the tempter and failing. He eats again of the tree of the knowledge of good and evil, but this time he is aware of his act and his weakness. He knows that by eating the fruit his power is crippled, he henceforth must act within the circle of good and evil, and not beyond it in the Nietzschean sense. Therefore, John Tanner struggles—struggles desperately for freedom, honour, self, one and indivisible—all to no avail. He is captured by the Life Force in the guise of a woman.

That is the new being Shaw has made, or rather the natural fact he has discovered and interpreted. He has symbolised instinct directed by will at the dawn of the conscious-

ness of its own innate power. He has flashed this idea upon the stage in a series of brilliant scenes, incidents, and personalities with a contempt for artistic tradition only possible in the master.

BERNARD SHAW.

1904

IV

THE PHILOSOPHER

Ana. Is there nothing in Heaven but contemplation, Juan?

Don Juan. In the Heaven I seek, no other joy. But there is the work of helping life in its struggle upward. Think of how it wastes and scatters itself, how it raises up obstacles to itself and destroys itself in its ignorance and blindness. It needs a brain, this irresistible force, lest in its ignorance it should resist itself. What a piece of work is man! says the poet. Yes: but what a blunderer! Here is the highest miracle of organisation yet attained by life, the most intensely alive thing that exists, the most conscious of all the organisms; and yet, how wretched are his brains! Stupidity made sordid and cruel by the realities learnt from toil and poverty: Imagination resolved to starve sooner than face these realities, piling up illusions to hide them, and calling itself cleverness, genius! And each accusing the other of its own defect: Stupidity accusing Imagination of folly, and Imagination accusing Stupidity of ignorance: whereas, alas! Stupidity has all the knowledge, and Imagination all the intelligence.—*Man and Superman*, Act iii, pp. 105-6.

IV

THE PHILOSOPHER

WHILST not despising his own power as an artist, Bernard Shaw rightly looks upon himself as a philosopher. That is to say, he has a clear and ordered conception of life and the relationship of its various parts. Such a type of mind has never been properly valued in Britain except in a very superficial way: we value the moralist more than the philosopher. This may be a national form of self-appreciation, a kind of racial egotism; we are all moralists more or less. No philosopher could be popular under such circumstances, for by the very nature of his calling he would tend to disturb the habitual peace of mind incidental to moral certitude. And few human beings like having their habits disturbed.

True philosophy is never far removed from

criticism. It is really the critical habit of mind expressing itself in terms of life. It is a constant arranging and rearranging of the details of life, and is as bewildering and varied as these are. Or, rather, it is as varied as the perceptive faculty is quick to receive and apply impressions of life. A great store is set upon originality in such matters. But originality matters very little and very fortunately, because there is very little of it, especially in the world of ideas. What does matter is the force of its application—the vividness of its portrayal. Individuality of expression, not novelty, is originality.

It is the business of the philosopher to be engaged, not so much with his own ideas, as with finding expression for those ideas necessary to his age, which have not yet been adequately expressed in the terms of his era. The philosopher is the interpreter of an age. He tells you what you mean. He translates the dreams, thoughts, and aspirations of an age into the currency of common thought. And by doing this he indicates fresh lines of

The Philosopher

action. Were it not for him the wheel of progress would remain stationary. Bernard Shaw, the philosopher, sees the wheel of the modern social wagon stuck in a deep rut and the driver and passengers quite indifferent. Having a keen sense of natural laws, he knows very well that if they don't wake up and move along, the wheels will become rotten and the whole thing fall to pieces. So with much concern, being a kind-hearted man, he starts, with generous intent, to criticise—that is, in English, to insult the passengers. And after much endeavour he has made so much of an impression that some of them have actually got out of the wagon and put their shoulders to the wheel. That is what Shaw wants. He does not say, " Hitch your wagon to a star," but " Put your shoulder to the wheel."

Bernard Shaw's originality, among modern philosophers at least, lies in the closeness with which his ideas are related to society itself. I mean not the sameness, but the organic relationship which exists between his ideas and the actions of ordinary men and women. His

Bernard Shaw

concepts are like a running commentary upon the doings of his fellows. This is brought out very clearly in the apt use he makes of personal experience and personal observation, both in his essays and in his lectures and conversation. The last, indeed, is largely composed of humorously annotated reminiscences.

This difference is one of the chief causes of his many incisions into popular conventions and the consequent intellectual bloodshed. So long as a philosopher remains abstracted from intimate relations with the doings of his kind ; so long as he theorises broadly and learnedly ; so long will he be quite safe from doing harm or good. But once let him apply his ideas to daily affairs and trouble, not necessarily advantageous, may be expected. For it is possible that a philosopher who is alive to modern needs may set society on the wrong track, but it is quite certain he will set it by the ears. The point is, however, that philosophy, like art, is vital only when it is applied to life. That is Bernard Shaw's position ; he is vital to the age, to the hour, because his

The Philosopher

ideas are constantly coming in touch with the everyday affairs.

This is brought out in his plays and elaborated in his prefaces. He seems always to be dealing with the immediate destiny of men and women with a desire to frustrate the workings, not only of a wasteful social system, but of destiny itself, or rather, to put human beings in such a position as to leave the final word with them, and not with the unknown. Unlike Ibsen's plays, which depict and symbolise the net of convention and destiny in which all men are caught, interpreting a dramatic idea which realises the dawning of a conscious struggle with this appalling tyranny, Bernard Shaw's plays give us a picture of men and women just a little more advanced in the scale of consciousness. His characters have tasted with more appreciation the fruit of the tree of knowledge of good and evil. They not only taste, but are inclined to enjoy. Shaw's philosophy is the expression of this attitude towards life. It is an attitude which, if not exactly beyond good and evil, is at least beyond

any good and evil other than that which is generated in the individual. Bernard Shaw is a philosophic missioner. He has the preaching habit in an extreme degree. Indeed, with another turn of the wheel, it is quite thinkable, he might have been saving souls instead of brains——and possibly he is already doing so.

The central idea in his philosophy is the conception of the underlying energy of life as the world-will. He has conceived this as a force—the Life-force, as he calls it—eternally seeking expression by instruments of greater certainty and power. His closeness to reality and his insistence upon the concrete has made this view of things free from what is obscure and shadowy. At the same time, his clear conception of the Life-force as the creative will of the universe is profoundly mystical. Shaw as a thinker must indeed be classed with the more practical of the mystics. He has a similar outlook, and a like insistence upon immediate action, a lively hatred of doing nothing and of arguing about nothing.

The Life-force must not be imagined as

The Philosopher

standing apart from ordinary things. It is neither an outside and independent deity nor a metaphysical toy. On the contrary, the Life-force has for Shaw no other existence than that of living things. Just as there is no such thing as poverty, but only poor people ; just as there is no such thing as happiness, but only happy beings ; or no such thing as beauty, but only beautiful things ; so for Shaw there is no such final and complete thing as the world-will, but only a world willing itself towards ampler certainty of its end. By this attitude he escapes the pitfalls of the god-idea which have crippled the world since the dawn of history.

The Life-force is of no use even to itself— granting it has a separate existence—without organisms ; for it is by the energy of these specialised parts towards newer specialisations that it has its being. Bernard Shaw conceives the pageant of life as an evolution whose final consummation is not man, but whose progress is towards a fuller and a deeper realisation of its own purpose and aim. The universe

for him is nothing less than a series of magnificent experiments made by the Life-force with the object of creating for itself an all-powerful, all-intelligent medium for its own expression.

Man is no more final in this series of experiments than the starfish or the ape were final. If that had been the aim of life, surely the result were not worth the trouble; for, after all, there is very little real difference between man and what man is pleased to call the lower animals. The differences in many ways are disadvantageous to man. For instance, that very little difference in the brain of man which has made all the difference in the world between him and the animals, whilst giving man a keener consciousness of joy, has also given him a deeper capacity of sorrow. The difference is between a frank and unthinking acceptance of life and a contemplative, a reflective, a self-conscious acceptance of life.

Of the two, the simple acceptance of life peculiar to the animals is more amenable to the Life-force than its self-conscious fellow.

The Philosopher

What does not consciously resist is naturally more plastic. And so long as the highest forms of life were content to shut their eyes and open their mouths, and be thankful for the small mercies of the universe, a certain progress was made. Shaw does not look upon this progress, or evolution, as consecutive and assured. He thinks it highly probable that the Life-force has made many a faulty experiment. If, as he truly points out, man is a blunderer, what must we call the Life-force for creating man ?

The whole of life is wrapped up in this as yet inscrutable question. It is probable, as Shaw points out, there is a shaping force immanent in life, and both informing and needing concrete things ; a force that can only have its will when these beings are able to take their will. But until then it is a blind force, powerful enough to mould the stuff of life into working shapes, tendril, tentacle, claw, hand, or what not, but all issuing in a series of cosmic experiments, on an infinite scale of seemingly prodigal wastefulness, with no defi-

nite idea as to results. Time, matter, energy spent and re-spent, formed and re-formed. Æons of time in which Life's highest expression was realised in an eye at the end of an antenna. Æons of time in which the eye became the window of a brain that could not reason. And still further, æons in which the eye was still the look-out of a brain, but of a brain, as in man, with the divine gift of reason —a gift which has never from the day of its creation to the present been able to explain one of the mysteries that were inscrutable at its inception.

Shaw still has faith in this mysteriously blundering world-will much in the same way as people used to have faith in a god. But there is this important difference, the recognition that whatever may be the aim of the Life-force, it can never attain it, not only without man, but without the series of experiments that have led up to man. In fact, Life is so needful of man that the only worthy thing for man to do is to help Life in its struggle upward ; to prevent a repetition or continuance

The Philosopher

of all this waste of energy and material that has proceeded through the ages of ignorance and blindness : the dark ages of creation in which Life struggled to create a being that would be able to carry on her work with intelligence and power.

It is gradually becoming obvious, even to rational people, that intelligence without will, on the one hand, is just as useless as will without intelligence, on the other. What man needs is a combination of the two—always understanding intelligence as a knowledge of the aim of life, and will as the desire to carry it out. In *Man and Superman*, Don Juan takes quite a compassionate view of life, and not without reason. Any recognition of a wasteful process brings something like feelings of compassion, especially when the intention of the process-wielder is imagined to be a good one, as must be the case in reference to life, otherwise we should all go insane ; for it is quite possible to look upon the universe as a series of remediable errors and remain sane. It is possible, also, to be both sane and in-

different to, or ignorant of, the purpose of life. But it is not possible to keep mentally balanced before the awful idea of a world irrevocably and eternally wrong. Don Juan, who is, in this reference at all events, Bernard Shaw, is quite sane in his compassionate admission of the blundering of the Life-force; and he is doubly sane in allowing compassion to take the practical course of desiring to help the blind thing on its upward struggle.

But it must not be imagined that there is any more piety in this wish than the piety that is to be found in desire as a motive force. Don Juan has no more desire to save the world for the world's sake than the world has any desire to save Don Juan for Don Juan's sake. His end is purely selfish, for he sees nothing more in his own desire for something finer, than the working of the world's desire for something better. "I tell you," he says, "that as long as I can conceive something better than myself I cannot be easy, unless I am striving to bring it into existence or clearing the way for it. That is the law of my life.

The Philosopher

That is the working within me of Life's incessant aspiration to higher organisation, wider, deeper, intenser self-consciousness, and clearer self-understanding."

This attitude is more allied with primal nature than with any conscious endeavour of man. Bernard Shaw seems to find a new language for nature, or rather a new language for the evolutionary theory. He definitely and, unlike most philosophers, without apology, places man in the procession of life. He treats man as an animal having brains and self-consciousness. He considers him in reference to will, and his will in reference to the will of the universe. But note that it is in reference and not deference to it. For once man awakens to a lively sense of his position in the world he must needs face life purged of all deference to any other tradition than that which ministers to his needs. Shaw is such a man : he is in revolt not only against man's way of looking at life, but against life's way of treating man.

And if we face the facts of life we have soon to admit that this is the only sane atti-

tude to take. Man for ages has been on his knees. He has been thanking his gods and cringing before the unknown fates, as though, on the one hand, they had given him a great bounty at considerable sacrifice to themselves, and, on the other, as though he could only propitiate them by renouncing what little of the more or less problematical good things of life he ever possessed. He rarely imagined himself the injured party. Even when this happened, as in the case of Schopenhauer, he did not imagine that life was the remedy, but death. The persistence of the will to live in the face of the eternal and blind pain of life could only be counteracted by the resistance, the negation of the will.

This, on the face of it, was a sounder and braver view of life than that which looked to salvation by atonement and vicarious sacrifice —its active negation of the will to live was at least impossible without a supreme use of the will to power. If the will to live were to be combated by the will to die, it was a combat that would have glorified and justified its

The Philosopher

cause. But the acceptance of the will to live on no other condition than that one should be rewarded in some other phase of consciousness for all the shortcomings of this, presents nothing for the future but a dreary waste of sameness and increasing stupidity. Such a state of things can, however, never be complete. No matter how much he may try to agree with God, or Life, or the Universal Will, or whatever he may call the Unknown, unless he knows what he is doing, unless he acts with a will that can dominate the brain ; until that neglected organ can see at least a few steps ahead, the Unknown will use him again and again, as it has done in the past, as the material of experiments of whose success past records do not give us any cause for enthusiasm.

Man has really very little to be " thankful for." True, there is much in the world that amuses him, and much that affords him, more or less, satisfying occupation. But, after all and behind all, there is the fatality of ignorance and incapacity, and their children folly

and waste, or worse, contentment and indifference. If there is one sin in the present stage of evolution it is contentment. No human being can afford to be contented; and if he be so, his sin will surely track him down. Our poverty-stricken and chaotic consciousness is reflected in our material affairs—in our hopelessly ugly cities, in our starvation, and in our disease. And just as the humility and contentment of the poor are bringing the grey hairs of civilisation in sorrow to the grave, so the contentment of man, in the face of the mystery of life and the limits of human power, is reducing him to an ineffectual organism which ultimately must be scrapped by Nature, or the Life-force, as the outworn medium of a worthless experiment.

This certainly would happen to man were it not for the few intrepid spirits who, from age to age, restore to the flagging spirit of the races some new energy—a Shelley, for instance, who was by no means the ineffectual angel, beating in the void his luminous wings in vain, of the circumspect and academic

mind of Matthew Arnold. Shelley beat his luminous wings in vain no more than William Blake did, nor, for the matter of that, Ibsen, or Nietzsche, or Shaw. For these, in the realm of religion and philosophy, are the vitalisers of mankind. The vanity of their endeavours is the illusion of those who happen to be too near them. Bernard Shaw is in this line of descent. But he is by no means derivative except in the broadest sense ; he probably owes more to Shelley, Blake, the scientists Erasmus Darwin, and Lamarck, than to either Ibsen or Nietzsche, to whom his philosophy has been frequently attributed. Truth needs no label, and it does not matter whether Shaw's philosophy is consciously derivative or not. Any philosophy that is enunciated in a way that can attract the attention of thoughtful people must stand or fall on the validity of its thesis, and not on its authority.[1]

[1] As an historical point, Shaw was as surely Ibsenite in his early novels before he had read Ibsen, as he was undoubtedly feeling his way to a similar point of view, which years afterwards he discovered in Friedrich Nietzsche. But such speculations matter very little. Shaw is one of those

Bernard Shaw

The attitude of such minds is always complexioned with a certain insolence of bearing. They are irreverent of the old gods, and are the first to laugh at the new. But Bernard Shaw comes not as a god-breaker, but rather as a god-maker. This is where his philosophy joins hands with religion. He arrives in civilisation at a moment when men have no longer any very moving faith in a living God. Jehovah is dead, and the God of Sundays is dying. Many substitutes have been tried instead of them, but there has been a tin-pot ring about their voices which has not stirred

representatives of spiritual energy who, by stimulating the intelligence of their age, even by the inverse process of causing it to resist them, actually save the world. Since the above was written, however, Shaw has himself lodged a protest against the growing habit of attributing every view he utters "outside the range of an ordinary suburban churchwarden" as derived from Neitzsche, Strindberg, Ibsen, or others; and, in the *Preface to Major Barbara*, he has given the names of some of the actual authors who have influenced him. It is indeed a strange list, including Charles Lever (in an almost forgotten story entitled, *A Day's Ride : A Life's Romance*); Captain Wilson, author of a metaphysical system called *Comprehensionism;* Samuel Butler, Ernest Belfort Bax, and Mr. Stuart-Glennie.

214

men either to exaltation or to depravity. It has just left them where they were.

Shaw comes as a heretic among the children of the modern faith in convention, in precedent, in the institution. He does not deny the existence of their gods, for he knows them to be only too real. Neither does he advise their return to a faith in the gods that are no more. "Beware of the man whose god is in the skies," he says, knowing quite well how, since the beginning of the record of man's doings, the sky-god has been the arbiter of a destiny which can never lead aright. Because, until man has become the arbiter of his own destiny, he can never realise the purpose of the world.

It has too readily been supposed that the purpose of the world is to serve and perfect man; but Bernard Shaw has consistently put this conception on one side in favour of its direct opposite. So far from the Life-force having as its highest purpose the salvation of man, he supposes, as we have seen, that the highest purpose of man is to realise the trend

of the Life-force. And only to the extent that man becomes in this way the saviour of the world is man of value. Consistently with this idea he views the possible failure and extinction of man with optimistic fortitude, for he knows that such a contingency could only be the result of man's failure to take the opportunity given him of realising the aim of the world. But man is not an end in himself. The Life-force is not spending itself in perfecting so limited an instrument for its purpose. Man in the natural course of events must be surpassed; he is no longer looked upon as an end, but as a means to an end. He is as much a creature of transition as any species in the order of the universe. On this conception Bernard Shaw bases not only his distinctive criticism of man, but his constructive idea of the Superman.

It cannot be said that Shaw's philosophy is a bridge between the ideas of man and Superman. But it is an indication of the direction. His critical aim is an endeavour to eradicate all those tendencies in man that militate against

The Philosopher

Superman. For Superman is his conception of the procession of the species at the point when the Life-force shall have found an efficient instrument for carrying out its purpose. And all Shaw's constructive proposals are designed to lead man towards Superman, from blind and imperfect subjection to conscious co-operation with the Life-force.

Nothing illustrates this better than his conception of Duty. "Duty," he says, "is what one should never do." Considered in the light of the rest of his philosophy, it will be readily understood that he does not mean to substitute anarchy for duty. Shaw is just as much opposed to social anarchism as nature is to chaos. There is, indeed, no such thing as anarchy in nature, and for the same reasons there can be no such thing as anarchy in social life. The Life-force grows out of order following upon right action. And a proper conception of Shaw's negation of duty is impossible without some idea of what he would consider right action.

His repudiation of duty makes it clear that

right action is not something following upon
authoritative concepts. It does not spring
out of "ought" or "should." And, on the
other hand, his negation of all formulas—
"The golden rule is that there are no golden
rules"—makes for the abolition of all arbi-
trary distinctions in such considerations. It
actually throws the source of action upon the
individual. Instead of saying to man, as the
moralists did, "Do what you ought to do," he
says, "Do what you want to do." It is the
directly opposite doctrine to that enunciated
by Carlyle. His "Do the Duty which lies
nearest thee, which thou knowest to be a
Duty," becomes "The repudiation of Duty
is the first step towards progress." For, as
Bernard Shaw points out in *The Quintessence of
Ibsenism*, "Duty arises at first, a gloomy
tyrant out of man's helplessness, his self-
mistrust, in a word, his abstract fear. He
personifies all that he abstractly fears as God,
and straightway becomes the slave of his duty
to God. He imposes that slavery fiercely on
his children, threatening them with hell, and

punishing them for their attempts to be happy. When, becoming bolder, he ceases to fear everything, and dares to love something, this duty of his to what he fears evolves into a sense of duty to what he loves. Sometimes he again personifies what he loves as God; and the God of Wrath becomes the God of Love: sometimes he at once becomes a humanitarian, an altruist, acknowledging only his duty to his neighbour. This stage is correlative to the rationalist stage in the evolution of philosophy and the capitalist phase in the evolution of industry. But in it the emancipated slave of God falls under the dominion of Society, which having just reached a phase in which all the love is ground out of it by the competitive struggle for money, remorselessly crushes him until, in due course of further growth of his spirit or will, a sense at last arises in him of his duty to himself. And when this sense is fully grown, which it hardly is yet, the tyranny of duty is broken; for now man's God is himself; and he self-satisfied at last ceases to be selfish."

Just as in the past creeds and theologies have been thrown overboard, so must succeeding generations establish their growth by repudiating and casting on one side those beliefs and morals which in their turn have served what purpose they ever had. Sometimes they have served no further purpose than indicating, by the fact of their existence, that the course of life is not infallibly progressive — that the Life-force makes errors, and occasionally runs into a blind alley, from which there is no way out but by a return along the path traversed, until the vital thread of life is picked up again. And this is just what Bernard Shaw advocates. He says in effect that man is an evolutionary *cul de sac*— that he has progressed as far as he can along the human track. He is a link in the chain of evolution only in so far as the Life-force has found him necessary as an experiment, and it is false science and false philosophy to legislate and look upon man as something final and established. Yet just because he is an experiment in life, he is of the procession moving

The Philosopher

towards what is greater than himself. That is why it is necessary for him to retrace his steps towards the place where he may resume the aim of life with the added power which has come through the experiences of his detour. Any other view than this were illusion, as man's belief in the suspension of his faculties at death and their resumption afterwards in bliss or torment, according to how much of his life has been spent in deference to entirely human concepts of a God and a God's love and hatred. Or, on the other hand, the repudiation of this idea of man as a transition towards something that shall surpass man more greatly even than man surpasses the ape, as well as that of God, were rank pessimism whose logical end is the negation of the will to live.

But the repudiation of the will to live will never be popular even with the best minds because of the limitations of our knowledge of the life we would destroy. What is Life ? were as difficult a question to answer as Pilate's 'What is Truth ?' The philosophy

of Bernard Shaw is a plea for more light on this subject. His theory of the negation of duty is but a phase of his argument, a convenient vantage point to view the whole. At the same time, it is the quintessential word of his philosophy, because in the repudiation of duty we are at once thrown back upon those passions and desires which it has been the whole aim of civilisation to keep in bond. Does Shaw advocate the loosening of these bonds—the freeing of the animal instincts? The answer to this question is, that he does. Bernard Shaw actually teaches a doctrine which, in spite of his no formula protestation, has at least one golden rule—Do what you want to do.

Such a doctrine, whilst taking the risks of licence, does not necessarily involve humanity in one great debauch, as pious and timid people are fond of imagining. But even if it did, that would be no argument against the doctrine; for, providing we cannot have a race of men so self-powered as to be able to resist destructive desires, it were better that

The Philosopher

humanity should annihilate itself as quickly as possible in one great orgie. But this would be impossible—it would be nothing short of a denial of the will to live. And the very essence of the doctrine of a desire-directed life is, that rather than denying life it takes up the cause of life at its most vital point—the instinctive and unconquerable will to live. To do what you want to do is to ally yourself with the Life-force.

The thing people have to get out of their minds is that desire is coincident with vice. It is nothing of the sort. Vice is that which makes for the destruction of some form of life, and, like virtue, it is its own reward; but, like virtue again, it has no value, unless it be the result of personal choice—of desire, in short. Bernard Shaw sees quite clearly that mere voluptuousness can have but one end— the destruction of power. That is seen daily in the civilised form of desire surreptitiously expressing itself behind a moral code. Shaw has, indeed, called himself a Puritan in the old sense, and he distinctly says that the volup-

tuary will have to be eliminated from the evolutionary process.

Ever since that incident occurred in life which produced man a battle has been going on between the result of the incident—man— and the probably unwitting cause of it— nature, alias the Life-force. At one point in the course of evolution the highest form of sentient matter—man—commenced to think about itself. Self-consciousness was born. The Life-force as exemplified in the mind of man became a mirror in which man saw himself. The vision pleased him so well that he has done practically nothing ever since but gaze and admire. Man has become an obsession. Civilisation, instead of being an aid to the creation of new and greater forms of life, has simply been an expedient for allowing humanity to live upon its self-reputation.

From the instant man became obsessed by his own beauty and wisdom evolution ceased. If it had been possible for the apes to have acquired this conceit, evolution would have ceased with them just the same. Now, Shaw's

The Philosopher

advocacy of a return to the instinctive life is the recognition that the only genuine motive force of life lies in instinct. So long as the instincts were followed life evolved higher forms. Man, by substituting duties for instincts, has actually sterilised life's power of growth—has thrown the Life-force into the necessity of having to perpetually repeat the same forms instead of creating new ones.

It is not, however, new forms for the sake of novelty that are demanded, but new forms for the sake of new capacity. The point at which the Life-force became ineffectual was the point at which instinct was limited by morality. Man, by attempting to suppress the world-will, which is another name for instinct, has come nearer to the negation of life than any other species. Bernard Shaw, recognising desire, instinct, and will to be nothing less than the Life-force itself, advocates as boldly as Nietzsche advocates, and with much greater clearness, acceptance of the fact. For by this means alone can we hope for Superman.

But Shaw and Nietzsche have few other

resemblances. Bernard Shaw's Superman is quite a social person, whereas Nietzsche's is but an abstraction—a great idea, but not a concrete conception. There is a benevolence in Shaw never found in Nietzsche. Shaw is human, Nietzsche—superhuman. That is why Shaw sees the Superman in Shakespear, in Goethe, in Shelley—who are not, in the Nietzschean sense, Supermen at all. Man, according to Nietzsche, will be surpassed : "*I teach you Superman.* Man is a something that shall be surpassed. What have ye done to surpass him ? All beings hitherto have created something beyond themselves : and are ye going to be the ebb of this great tide and rather revert to the animal than surpass man ? What with man is the ape ? A joke or a sore shame. Man shall be the same for Superman, a joke or a sore shame."

What Shaw calls Superman, Nietzsche would rightly call man. Leaving Shakespear out of the question as being too abstract for our purpose, and taking Shaw's other examples of the Superman—Goethe, Shelley,

The Philosopher

Napoleon, and Cromwell—we find that, great as these men are, they do not accord very well with the Nietzschean conception of Superman. They are powerful and great in many ways—but human-all-too-human. They would probably be of Nietzsche's chosen order, which must come into existence before Superman can be born. Shaw says that, " Until there is an England in which every man is a Cromwell, a Rome in which every man is a Cæsar, a Germany in which every man is a Luther plus a Goethe, the world will be no more improved by its heroes than a Brixton villa is improved by the pyramid of Cheops. The production of such a nation is the only real change possible to us." But, according to Nietzsche, the production of such a nation would be only the preliminary step towards Superman. Shaw's nation of Supermen is but the realisation of the great noon of Zarathustra, when man stands in the middle of his course between animal and Superman : it is not the actual day, but " the way unto a new morning."

Bernard Shaw

Shaw's conception of man aiding the Life-force in the struggle towards a superhuman world, whatever form Superman may ultimately take, is Don Juan's conception of Heaven as a contemplative state in which the human being becomes conscious of itself. There is something in this idea closely allied to the basis of all religious aspiration. Shaw seems to have gone back not only to the Greek philosophic concept "Know Thyself," but to the still older concept of divine immanence. But he differentiates his own philosophy from those of the past when he allies the God within with the Life-force, and the Life-force with Instinct. It is impossible to understand Shaw unless this is recognised. His negation of ideals and formulas is part of his endeavour towards the rehabilitation of the Life-force as instinctive action which formula has always sought to either curb or destroy. At the same time, it must not be concluded that, because of this desire to place instinct in its true perspective, Shaw would advocate the wilder forms of action usually

The Philosopher

associated in the popular mind with instinct. His philosophy, of course, takes this risk, because he knows, just as Nietzsche knew when he wished to take up the tradition of growth in Europe where it was dropped by the Greeks of the Periclean era, that evolution proceeding only out of instinct is necessarily a revolutionary factor.

But just as his theory of the repudiation of institutions is consistent with social evolution so his philosophy of no formula is consistent with individual growth. The one is the corollary of the other. The imposition of morals upon the individual will at first frustrates, then limits, and finally subjugates it. The result is that undesirable state in which we find the majority of civilised people to-day—a state in which the constant suppression of all intimations of will has reduced the races to habitual spiritual apathy. This habit practically amounts to a denial of life, for we have seen that instinct, will, and the Life-force are synonymous terms. The whole theory of moral order is an attempt to conserve the

power of life, to prevent that prodigality of creative instinct which in unordered nature looks like waste. But man's attempt to improve upon this method of the Life-force has failed, because he has never been certain of what the Life-force wanted. He is only occasionally certain of what he wants himself, especially in that emphatic way which would ultimately result in his getting it. Shaw has said that what the Life-force is endeavouring to evolve for itself is a brain, and man has evidently had some intuition of this; for he has taken his brain so seriously that he has quite overlooked its limitations. Reason has been accepted, just as morals have been accepted, as an end in itself. Once this position was taken it was quite natural that the next step should have been the negation of anything that did not spring from reason, and as reason is not creative the limitation of creativeness followed.

Shaw, recognising the errors of the age of reason, advocates the era of the will. Just as we must look upon the institutions as the tools

The Philosopher

of a generation to be discarded or improved upon by succeeding generations, so must we recognise that the intellect and its methods of expression are, in the same way, means of life, and not ends in themselves. The desire of the Life-force for brains should be met by man, not by the indifference of reason eternally looking back at itself, but by the concentration of the mind upon the blindness of life, urging forward towards the light. This is the contemplative attitude; it is the attitude of co-operation with life for the sake of living, in the sense that living is growth, creation; and growth and creation are power, wisdom, joy.

Generally speaking, few would disagree with such a doctrine. Probably all men mean the same thing, although it works out differently in practice: just as all the leaves on a tree desire to be leaves, and all are leaves, but no two are alike. The differences are similar to the differences in the fibre of the mind of man. Bernard Shaw has one great underlying idea which will always exonerate him from cynicism, just as his compassion with suffering

beings exonerates him from the charge of callous intellectualism : it is his belief that what man wants man can get. This is the highest compliment ever paid to man, and is, properly speaking, the quintessence of Shaw.

Man evolves, just as other species have evolved, not by natural selection, but by a constant satisfaction of his needs. Environment is in a perpetual state of flux, being modified and enhanced according to the needs of life's most powerful units. Man, having a brain and the means of contemplating his experiences, and thereby transferring them from the realm of blindly groping evolution to that of conscious experiment, has greater power for adapting materials to his ends than any other species. Therefore, it is the business of man to become conscious of the aim of life by contemplation and experiment. He must not seek the fruits of action, but action itself. Beauty and Happiness are by-products. He must satisfy his needs, and by doing so he will realise the will of the universe. But if this great discipline of taking the line of instinct,

which is by no means the line of least resistance, destroys the individual, nature's ends
are best served by his destruction. The ends
of life are remote. That which survives does
so only by power and joy : by action that can
face all conflicts without resentment and all
consequences without regret. The Life-force
only needs that which can save itself—that
which can save itself not by conserving, but by
spending itself, until light-hearted and free,
the self neither fore-doomed nor fore-ordained,
realising the full purpose of life, makes that
purpose his own.

p 142

PRINTED BY
WILLIAM BRENDON AND SON, LTD.
PLYMOUTH

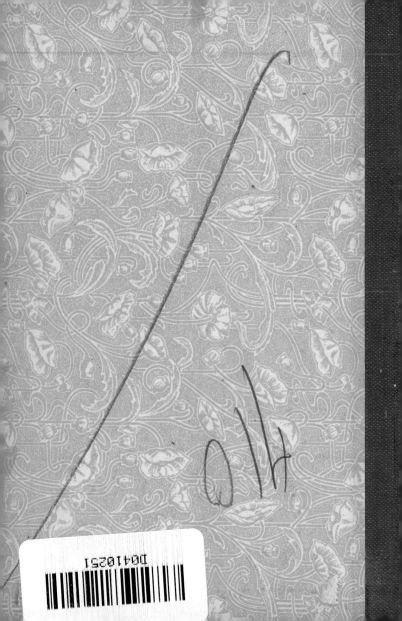